The Clue to Pascal

The Clue to

PASCAL

by
EMILE CAILLIET

Foreword
by
JOHN A. MACKAY

KENNIKAT PRESS
Port Washington, N. Y./London

201
c134e   SLM

223984

THE CLUE TO PASCAL

CONTENTS

PREFACE

ARISING as it does from the text of a short series of lectures delivered at the Institute of Theology at Princeton Theological Seminary during the summer of 1943, this book had to be limited in scope. Certain periods of Pascal's life and work could not be studied in detail. The author aimed rather at striking that keynote in the treatment of Pascal which appeared to him to be best sustained by honest study.

Rehandling the whole subject in the light of recent research, the author was impressed by the tremendous part the Bible played in the life and work of one of the profoundest thinkers of all time, and one of the greatest men of God who ever lived. Here, to him, is the clue to Pascal.

In the treatment of source material throughout this volume controversy has been avoided as far as feasible. The scholarly-minded will find in the appended notes the textual evidence upon which the author based his statements. This accounts for the lengthy form of these notes, which are arranged separately under the several chapters. It is hoped that they will furnish the reader with incentive for further study of Pascal. A book should be, not a grave, but a cradle.

The word *Œuvres* refers to the standard edition : *ŒUVRES DE BLAISE PASCAL publiées suivant l'ordre chronologique avec documents complémentaires, introductions et notes, par Léon Brunschvicg, Pierre Boutroux et Félix Gazier, " Les Grands Ecrivains de la France," Hachette, Paris.*

In this edition the *Pensées* appeared as Volumes 12, 13, and 14, edited by Léon Brunschvicg and published in 1904. Volumes 1, 2 and 3, containing the writings of Pascal and those of his relatives up to the *Mémorial* of November 23, 1654, appeared four years later. In editing these writings Brunschvicg followed a chronological order. Pierre Boutroux, who had collaborated with Brunschvicg in editing the mathematical works included in these volumes, and Félix Gazier were largely responsible for the edition of Volumes 4 to 11. In these eight volumes, containing the writings of Pascal and related documents from the date of the *Mémorial* to Pascal's death on August 19, 1662, Boutroux and Gazier followed the chronological method laid down by Brunschvicg. Boutroux had again edited all mathematical works, while Gazier had been responsible for the text and commentary on all other writings. The fourteen volumes of the complete edition, therefore, follow one chronological scheme.*

For the *Pensées*, in this complete edition, Brunschvicg developed a scheme of classification. A Concordance will be found in *Œuvres*, v. **12**, cclxxvi–ccciv, which gives for each fragment the corresponding reference to the original manuscript No. 9202, the first copy No. 9203, the second copy No. 12449, to be found in the Bibliothèque Nationale in Paris (cf. *Œuvres*, v. **12**, iii ff.), and the editions of Port-Royal (1670), Bossut (1779), Faugère (1844), Havet (1852), Molinier (1877–1879), and Michaut (1896). Concerning these editions, see *Œuvres*, v. **12**, xiii–xl.

The author calls the special attention of the reader to the treatment of Scriptural references in the notes as well as in the text of this present work. *Since he was a Roman Catholic, Pascal used the Latin Vulgate*, which he often quoted from memory. He sometimes shortened the text as he quoted it, or added a commentary of his own where a text had been deleted. Sometimes he elaborated on a text, or combined several texts together. Occasionally he would translate directly from the original, with or without the help of other versions. In Chapter III, " A Lamp Unto My Feet," we discuss some of the problems raised by these habits of a writer whose mind was so thoroughly steeped in the Bible. *In his own discussions and for his quotations the author has regularly used the English version of the Vulgate, first published by the English College at Douay,* A.D. *1609, for Old Testament references; and the version first published by the English College at Rheims,* A.D. *1582, for New Testament references (John Murphy Company, Publishers, Baltimore, Maryland)*. The only exceptions to this rule occur in the Biblical texts used as mottoes at the beginning of each section where the King James, or Authorized Version, has been used.

The author wishes to express his profound gratitude to

* For every reference to the works of Pascal, the numerals in bold type indicate the volume, and the following numerals (Arabic or Roman) indicate the page. Thus *Œuvres*, v. **12**, 3 refers to Volume **12**, page 3 of the complete edition; and *Œuvres*, v. **12**, vi–viii refers to pages vi to viii of the same volume.

President John A. Mackay, of the Princeton Theological
Seminary, who invited him to give these lectures on Pascal
and the Bible. Meting out a Christian friendship so abounding, President Mackay has added his blessings to this little book
in the form of a Foreword cherished by author and reader alike.

Rev. Leonard J. Trinterud, of The Westminster Press, has
constantly encouraged the author to publish a series of Pascalian studies. His wise counsel and unfailing devotion continue to prove of great assistance through what is bound to
be a laborious undertaking.

Pressed by time, due to the demands of other publications
and of his professional duties, the author has had to rely on
Rev. Theodore C. Hume for the translation of a large part of
his material. Mr. Hume's wholehearted consecration to this
task and his resourcefulness in fine points of translation have
added much to this work, wherein a precious friendship has
been deepened.

Thanks must also be expressed to Professor William Shaffer
Jack, of the University of Pennsylvania, for his helpful sug-
gestions upon carefully reading over the pages of the last
chapter.

Part of the cost of the author's Pascalian research is being
covered by a grant from the special Research Fund of the
University of Pennsylvania. Grateful acknowledgment is here-
by extended to the members of the Faculty Research Committee
for their recognition of this endeavour.

E. C.

FOREWORD

SEVERAL things combine to give unusual significance to the publication of this book. To begin with, there is the unquestionable importance of the theme. Whatever relates to Pascal is important. His greatness as a man of science has been household knowledge for centuries. With his inventive genius are associated not a few mechanical devices, such as the barometer and the calculating machine, which have become part and parcel of our civilization. But it has not been so widely known that Blaise Pascal was as great a thinker in the realm of religion as he was in the realm of science. One even dares to say that in the generations to come his eminence as a Christian philosopher and saint will surpass his fame as a student of the natural order.

Two great names are linked together in the France of the seventeenth century : René Descartes and Blaise Pascal. Both were philosophers and men of science. Descartes, with his *Discourse on Method* and his famous dictum, " I think, therefore I am," became the father of modern philosophy. To-day we are crossing the threshold of an era, a tragic and hungry era, which begins to feel the inspiration, and is ready to accept the guidance, of the anguished Pascal more than that of the complacent Descartes. For the truth of a forgotten Pascalian dictum has become apparent : " The heart, too (the vital depths of human nature), has its reasons, which reason does not know." The new passion for the ultimately real rejects the epoch-making slogan of Descartes, preferring one which goes back through Pascal and Kierkegaard to Saint Paul, and which might be formulated thus : " I am thought, therefore I am." For real existence does not consist in the process of thinking, but in the act of finding oneself in God's great scheme of things. The thinker of the lineage of Pascal knows that it is not thought but moral decision that makes a man a true human spirit, opening up to the committed soul wide realms of reality which remain for ever veiled to the scrutiny of reason.

Few things are more significant than the present revival of

Pascal, and few will prove more beneficent in the history of contemporary thought. The reasons are obvious. Pascal anticipated intuitively facts about human nature and human life which our generation is learning by hard and doleful experience. His insight also into things divine was penetrating and deep, showing the only way to the "hidden God." At a time when thinkers were impressed with the unity of things, Pascal grasped and held life's basic antinomies. Where others saw simplicity, he sensed paradox. When man was being glorified afresh as "the measure of all things," he saw the beast as well as the angel in man. When the whole trend of thought was centrifugal, seeking ever wider generalizations for the formulation of truth, Pascal's thinking was centripetal; he sought not theories but facts; not universals but particulars. It was his quest of the concrete and real that led Pascal to the ultimate fact of existence, the fact of Jesus Christ, and to the most significant field of study in which the mind of man can engage, the world of the Bible.

This book is also important because it introduces us to the influence of the Bible upon the life and religious philosophy of Pascal. Blaise Pascal brought to the study of the Book the same acumen and intuitive genius that he had applied to the world of nature. No one has excelled him in formulating the unique character of the Bible and of the God whom the Bible reveals. Here is no God-idea, no God who is merely First Cause and Creator of harmony, no great Custodian of the moral order who confines His concern to rewarding the virtues and punishing the wicked. The God of the Bible is, as Pascal emphasized, the God of Abraham, of Isaac, and of Jacob, the God of Jesus Christ, the God who related Himself so closely to men of His choice whose lives He moulded, that He became their heritage, their deepest selves, becoming at length man in a Man. Pascal had proved in his experience that this God, the only living and true God, can never be known by men about whom the highest that can be said is that they are "wise people and scholars." God becomes known only to those who seek Him in an agony of desire, to seekers for whom Jesus Christ becomes luminous as the answer to life's deepest questions and needs. Such as have discovered in our time the new, strange world within the Bible amid the relativities of a chaotic world, and have founded their hope upon Jesus Christ and the historic Christian faith, will draw Pascal out of his own century into ours, and will find in him a leader and a road companion in the pilgrimage toward a better time.

No less significant is the fact that this book has been written by a layman. The author is a layman who exults in the fact that Pascal too was a layman. Emile Cailliet comes before the English-speaking public as one of an increasing group of laity in our time who are devoting themselves to religious thought and writing. This layman is also a scholar, one of the great authorities upon French language and literature, and a professor in one of the leading universities of the United States. Not the least valuable part of the book is the series of notes at the end. These bear the marks of true scholarship and will stimulate many a reader to make an excursion of his own into the vast and attractive field of Pascalian lore.

This leads one also to say that the author is a Frenchman, as might be supposed by his name. Professor Cailliet shares the enthusiasm of his countrymen for Pascal. He accepts the judgment that Pascal is the only man whom France can pit against the English Shakespeare. What is more significant still is that this Frenchman, without in any way minimizing the transcendent greatness of his hero, makes clear that the tragedy of Pascal was that he did not reach in his pilgrimage of thought the promised land toward which his deepest insights pointed the way. Very moving and tragic in their pathos are the last words of the writer: " Never was a Roman Catholic nearer evangelical Protestantism, nor farther away. In this supreme antinomy is summed up for us the secret of Pascal, and of his anguish."

There are some distinguished men in our time who have left their Protestant heritage and found in the Roman Catholic communion what appears to be to them a more adequate faith, and in Thomas Aquinas a luminous guide for their thinking. There are others, of whom the author of this book is one, who have left the Roman Catholic Church and found in the fellowship of evangelical Christians what their souls had vainly sought in the Roman tradition. In Blaise Pascal, more than in any other personality since the Reformation, we discover one whose life and thought provide a meeting-place where men of evangelical earnestness, whether Catholic or Protestant, may nourish their souls at the central spring of the Christian religion.   JOHN A. MACKAY.

PRINCETON THEOLOGICAL SEMINARY,
PRINCETON, N.J.

I. THE EMERGENCE OF A PILGRIM

Truth shall spring out of the earth. PSALM LXXXV. II

"GOD wills it! God wills it! God wills it! God wills it!"

The shout goes up from a thousand throats. Pope Urban II has just finished his sermon in the great square of Clermont "in the presence of four hundred bishops or mitred abbots, and of an immense gathering of the populace."[1] Forthwith each one of these breasts is marked with a cross of red cloth, and, without further tarrying, one hundred thousand poor folk fall into line under the leadership of Peter the Hermit. Eastward moves the endless column—toward the Danube Valley; toward the Bosphorus, where it will be cut to pieces by the Turks; on toward the Holy City, which at any cost must be set free. The nobles will follow later.

To this day, the memory of that uprising of a Christian people hovers over the vast, sloping square of Clermont; it stirs to life the robust, square outline of the basilica of Notre-Dame du Port, which for centuries has served as both church and citadel. This Romanesque structure, the greatest in all Auvergne, is buried like a huge cistern among the surrounding houses. Its sturdy bareness well bespeaks the character of the indomitable soul who reared its walls. Built of arkose, it is still quite light in colour, like all the older churches in Auvergne. It will be some time before the builders begin to use stone cut from the lava, which they will prefer because it is more durable. In those early days, however, a single structure—the Cathedral—leaps forth from the soil of Auvergne, with a single heavenward thrust, springing from a single-minded faith, its unobstructed eminence crowning the crest of the hill.

A Citadel of the Church

Riom belongs to the King, Montferrand to the Count. But Clermont belongs to the Bishop, and it is the Bishop's town which is thus dominated by the Cathedral. A walled town it is, embracing the mother church; the cloister; the abbey; the

13

Bishop's palace, with its gardens and chapel; the *officialité*; a prison; and cemeteries.²

Clermont is to remain a citadel of the Church, ruled by its bishops, from 1202 to 1551. Divided into the four parishes of Notre-Dame, la Cathédrale, Saint-Genès, and Saint-Pierre, the town also includes the convents of the Cordeliers and the Carmelite Friars, whose huge churches are thrown open to the crowds hungry for sermons. A ring of monasteries surrounds the town on every side: the Priory of Beaumont, the Chamalières' Chapter, the Minims of Saint-Pierre, the Augustinians, the royal abbeys of Saint-André and Saint-Alyre, the Barefooted Carmelite Friars of Chantoin, Jacobins, Ursulines.³ At the Cordeliers and at Saint-Alyre some relics from antiquity are to be seen.

This land of the Arvernes, where Vercingetorix, who led the Gauls against Cæsar, was born about 72 B.C., is the seat of a very ancient civilization. When the Bishop pays a visit to the great seminary at Montferrand, he passes through triumphal arches which bear inscriptions in Latin. At the Puy-de-Dôme, when the Observatory was being built, they found a statuette of the god Mercury, in the figure of a gay, strapping, young countryman, vigorous in appearance and with enormous fists. This ancient bronze piece was given a prominent place in the historical museum of Clermont, where Mercury stands to-day, in lieu of a patron saint, as it were, for this borderland of trade, watching over this industrious and practical folk who are at the same time basically religious in spirit.

The Gauls had a sanctuary here, the last stopping-place for pilgrims before they reached the sanctuary on the mountain. The Romans named the place Augustonemetum, the city of the Arvernes, and it finally became Clermont in the days of Pepin the Short. If the city of the Arvernes had become the Bishop's town, the real reason was that the bishops were originally leaders chosen by the people themselves. The high central ridge where these men were given authority stood as a kind of tangible evidence of the ever-surging movement of Christianity within the life of a race and of a region. "What bare strength, what powerful placidity was to be found in ancient Auvergne, sturdy of heart, vigorous with the blood of a great land lying between the four seas. Along with the solidity of your soil and tradition, along with gifts of nature and human wisdom, you possess impulsiveness, audacity and the folly of saintliness. High ridges have pushed their way up in the very heart of the plain, and volcanoes have burst forth, sundering apart the highlands."⁴

The primordial fire made Auvergne what it is, just as Auvergne, fashioned for a destiny surpassing its narrow bounds, made France what it is to-day. Something more than the geological history of France is recapitulated in this lofty region; in a sense it is the story of the whole world, and perhaps of its civilization. The flickering fires of a primitive culture, that of the Eyzie Grottoes, were first kindled in the valley of the Vézère, in Périgord. In this corner of France the record of our distant ancestors is inscribed in signs and symbols which are only now being deciphered with the aid of modern science. Of this process of unfolding the record of the past, Camille Julian says: "Every Frenchman who reveres his ancestors, every man who has a decent concern to know his own past, should make a pilgrimage to the Eyzies."⁵

The Mark of Calvinism

Shut in by its own highlands, overlooking the highways of civilization from afar, Auvergne finds its chief access to the outer world by way of the deep valley of the Limagne, which extends in a widening valley to the north. From the village of Gerzat, near Clermont in the Limagne valley, came the Bégon family, Blaise Pascal's forebears on his mother's side. Their family record has been traced back to the thirteenth century. Most of them were tillers of the soil; one was a priest, one a notary public. They were well received in local gatherings, and a written record has been preserved of their charitable gifts and of their habits of piety. Pascal's maternal grandfather, Victor Bégon, moved to Clermont toward the end of the sixteenth century and established himself as a merchant. The Pascal family also originated in the Limagne valley, where tradition associates them with the village of Cournon. They were a family of tradesmen—dealers in carts, perhaps—and they made their way up in the world by dint of unremitting toil. Under Louis XI, they were raised to the aristocracy, as members of the petty *noblesse de robe*. For several generations, the family had lived in Clermont, where Jean Pascal, great-grandfather to Blaise, was a *marchand bourgeois*. After making his fortune, he purchased the post of Inspector of Deeds, apparently rather late in life. His son, Martin Pascal, became Tax Collector for Clermont, and later Treasurer of the Bureau of Finance at Riom.⁶

Now it appears to be well established that Martin Pascal, grandfather of Blaise Pascal, was for a time a Calvinist. He was an independent thinker, and, as his grandson said of him, his opinions shifted freely " from *pro* to *con*." Like the grand-parents of Blaise Pascal, the Arnauld and the Lemaistre families were also of Huguenot descent, having had Protestant parents and earlier forebears, as Varin has shown.⁷ These facts throw a significant light on the development of Jansenism. They have quite a special relevance in our study of Pascal and the Bible. They may even help to shed new light on the problem concerning the versions of the Bible which Blaise Pascal may have used. Personally, we wonder whether he may not have found in the family library a copy of the Bible edited by the pastors and pro-fessors of the Church in Geneva, a printing of which was made by Thomas Portau, at Saumur, in 1614. We have come into personal possession of one such copy of the said printing, which served as family Bible, with the initial entry reading : " Mon père an 1560, il mourut 1619." Martin Pascal had great am-bitions for his son Etienne whom he sent to Paris to study law. There in the capital the latter doubtless felt the breath of the Renaissance, and it would be less than surprising to find this eager, self-taught man, with his encyclopædic mind, fingering through or even purchasing the Protestant edition of the Scrip-ture. His father had given him letters of introduction to the solicitor Arnauld, a brilliant leader of the Paris bar. Arnauld was the father of twenty children who became, as it were, the kindergarten for Port-Royal.

The Pascal family found itself threatened with persecution because of its Protestant leanings. Gaspard Montmorin de Saint-Hérem, Governor of Auvergne during the massacre of Saint Bartholomew's Day, received an order to put to death all Protestants within his jurisdiction. There were very few of them in fact, but the task was most unwelcome. He limited himself to having them all imprisoned. But when the town of Clermont was asked to aid in carrying out these arrests, it calmly decided, with that independence of spirit so admirable throughout its history, that integrity of character in its sons and citizens should take precedence over every other considera-tion. The Town Council decided, at its session of January 16, 1574, to seek a delay. The Governor insisted, and declared the town of Clermont to be ill-managed. A stern reprimand was given to the garrison commanders in Clermont, with instructions "to prepare at once a roll containing the name and surname of all those persons held under suspicion, with respect to religion." The town then hastened to send Lieutenant Textoris and one of the magistrates to the Governor to lay before him the serious reasons which the town of Clermont gave for not imprisoning those of its citizens who refused to recant. Saint-Hérem was apparently convinced, for at the session of the Town Council on January 30 it was decided simply to keep matters under surveillance, to read out the roll of names, and to file it at the close of the session. This roll of names may actually be seen among the municipal archives of Clermont, with the records of the corporate proceedings of the town in 1574, under date of January 30.

Among the names of those persons who took up, bore, and employed arms against the King in 1567 may be found the name of Anthoine Audigier, surnamed Le Peuchy, the name of some friends of the Pascal and Périer families. It should be recalled that Gilberte, elder sister of Blaise Pascal, later married Florin Périer. Among the names of those who did recant was that of Master Martin Pascal.[8] His grandson was also to face a bitter struggle within his own soul as he stood years later on the frontier of Roman Catholic orthodoxy. These sturdy souls were gifted with a freedom of spirit which made them critical of authority, if not rebellious against it. Small wonder it is then that we find Etienne Pascal, son of Martin and father of Blaise, protesting at the royal court in 1630 against the founding of a Jesuit college in Clermont.

A Garden in the Moat

Etienne Pascal was born in Clermont in 1588, eldest of a family of ten children. After pursuing the studies above referred to, he became *conseiller élu du Roy* in the electorate of Bas-Auvergne at Clermont. We shall have ample opportunity in these pages to become more fully acquainted with this perfect *honnête homme*, in the full sense of the word, a good Christian, slightly given to superstition as men were in those days, but in no sense a mystic. The strain of mysticism in his son Blaise came from his mother's side, a type of mysticism balanced by the common sense and realistic turn of mind so characteristic of this plebeian folk.

As magistrate at the Cour des Aides, Etienne Pascal would normally have made his home in Montferrand, seat of the High Court, but in 1616 he had married Antoinette Bégon, and in 1619 he had bought the Langhac mansion, close by the Abbey, in the Bishop's town.[9]

Let us now wend our way to the Pascal home. The good town of Clermont we enter by a gate leading us through the city wall. The wall is in poor enough repair, and in more than one' place it seems about to collapse. What was once a moat has been turned into a vegetable garden by the practical citizens of the neighbourhood. We shall need heavy boots, indeed, if we are to go up the narrow, winding alley, which is little better than a mass of mud. Let us hail a sedan chair! Huddled together on either side are tiny houses built of dark basalt, telling a tale of unrelieved penury. Opening upon the street are the windows of a small shop, letting in precious little sunlight through the heavy, half-closed shutters. On one side is the main door and the staircase, where a couple of tiny square windows give what light is needed. On the other side of the shop is the entrance into the cellar. Upstairs we find a single large room, with a low ceiling and wide casement window, and above that a tiny attic. That is all. The people of Auvergne know the meaning of poverty. Cut off from the other provinces by the lack of good roads, they import but little from beyond their own borders. On the other hand, the major part of their crops is consumed on the spot, sufficing for the needs of ordinary life, and even for some small degree of comfort, albeit upon a slender margin of monetary income.

This, in general, is the standard of life among the tradesmen of the main shopping streets, by which we entered Clermont. Their earnings, which would seem wretched to us, provide enough for upkeep, and enable them to receive and entertain their friends. Some of them have gallantly taken as their family motto the words : *Bene vivere et laetari*. A good living, as they see it, doubtlessly means just enough to treat one's friends for fifteen or twenty sous, and to buy a fine gown for a daughter's wedding. In the way of art there is hardly anything to speak of. Exteriors appear to mean little to the people of Clermont. Such painting as we find consists of a few portraits, while the only sculpture in the community is found inside a few of the more elegant homes. These folk are already living by Jansenist standards, even though the term has not yet been heard of.[10]

Along the Rue des Gras and the Rue des Chaussetiers are to be found a few mansions of moderate scale, but they offer little in the way of outward appointments. Here an ornate doorway, there a family crest carved above the lintel, indicate to the passer-by the owner's social standing. Except for the churches there is little to satisfy the sensitive eye. We enter the Gothic Cathedral, with its choir reminiscent of Beauvais. Perchance we shall find Antoinette kneeling in prayer, caught by a ray of sunlight flooding in rich colour through the resplendent stained glass.

The Pascal home is only a few steps from the Cathedral door, but we shall not find our way to it without some difficulty. Etienne Pascal does indeed live in the house at the corner of the Rue des Chaussetiers and the public square just south of the Cathedral, but he also occupies another house close by, opening on the Rue des Gras, the street named because of the steps by which it leads up to the very front of the Cathedral.[11] The fact is that the two houses are connected by a tiny court-yard, so that the Pascal family finds it easy to live in both houses at the same time.[12] The two houses once formed part of a huge, five-storied structure, built around a court, the Hôtel des Vernines, dating back about a hundred years. Etienne Pascal, being a practical man of affairs, had no sooner pocketed the title to the property than he remodelled the stables into a row of shops, which he rented out, and thus augmented the income which has made him one of Clermont's forty-three leading taxpayers.

Patriarchal Family Discipline

There it was that four children were born: Anthonia, in December, 1617, who died shortly after her baptism; on January 1, 1620, Gilberte, who was to become Madame Périer; on June 19, 1623, Blaise; and on October 5, 1625, Jacqueline.

Christened on June 27, 1623,[13] Blaise began life as a sickly child. He was barely a year old when he developed an alarming tendency to listlessness, and for months his life was feared for. Etienne was wild with anxiety. Believing the child to be the victim of an evil spell, he sought out the supposed enchantress, forced her to confess her crime, and made her transfer the spell to a black cat, which promptly expired! A poultice was applied to the wretched infant, made from nine leaves of three herbs gathered before sunrise by a seven-year-old child. Soon afterward Blaise was well again. Such evidences of superstition need not trouble us overmuch, for they were deeply rooted in the customs of the people, to whom they would not have appeared in the least out of the ordinary. We mention the incident merely to recall some of the trials which beset Etienne, and to note that Blaise, from his earliest years, was a victim of poor health. There is little doubt that he was already " given to intense, but balanced, hypersensitivity."[14] The phrase is borrowed from Jacques Chevalier, who goes on to add, however : " Despite the symptoms, evident from infancy, of some ailment which may have been congenital, Pascal never, at that time or later on, showed any sign of mental disorder or hysteria, nor of superstition on his part."[15] An inner flame, out of all proportion to his bodily strength, was already burning in the mind of Blaise.

The " very pious and very charitable " Antoinette died in 1626, leaving President Pascal alone to raise and train three children, all of them quite young. We must admire the understanding integrity and devotion which he brought to this task. As regards their formal education, it may well be said that genius is a matter of infinite patience. Nature never succeeds at a single bound in producing those happy phenomena we call geniuses and saints. Fitting indeed is the comment of Maurice Barrès, as he thought of Blaise Pascal and his father : " Our sons resemble our most profound thoughts."[16]

Young Blaise was " an only son, between two much-beloved sisters, now left without . . . a mother, to be brought up by a father who was a lonely and somewhat saddened man." More than likely it is that Blaise was " fondled and admired, as well as having to grow up under the shadow of this sorrow. Who can say what mark this may have left upon his later years? His imperious manner, his impatience with opponents, his extremely sensitive nature, his hasty temper, his inclination to sorrowful brooding. To his sisters he owed the feminine strain in his own nervous manner, and, no less, that grace and charm which won him so many devoted friends."[17]

What noble spirits they were, both of these sisters ! The elder, Gilberte, took her mother's place in the home, where she assumed a measure of responsibility beyond her years. Well she deserves the happy title " the Martha of the family," given her by Fortunat Strowski. Among the many who have written of her brother's life, Gilberte alone, according to Vinet,[18] truly understood that great soul. We shall refer often to her impressions in the following pages.[19] As for Jacqueline—or Jacquette, as she was called—who later entered a convent under the name of Sister Sainte-Euphémie, we may again recall Vinet's estimate : " As we think of her, we cannot withhold a feeling of admiration even more unqualified, and marked by more genuine respect, than for him [Blaise]. It is to be doubted whether we shall find anywhere a more accomplished character, in man or woman, than that of Jacqueline."[20]

As we look back at this family, one feature is strikingly evident, namely, the patriarchal tradition of family discipline. If the men and women of that period did not turn to the teachings of the Bible for precise guidance in the domain of politics, they accepted its authority unchallenged in the realm of family life, where patriarchal authority was sustained with the full force of law and custom.[21] However, this fundamental respect for patriarchal tradition did not in any way shut them from the new light of the Renaissance.

The New Light of the Renaissance

From the second floor of the Pascal mansion there opened a huge window, for the house was built in the sixteenth century, when men felt the need of more light to read by. It was a century that opened many windows of the mind! This style of residence was common among Clermont families of standing equal to that of Etienne Pascal, for if there was little in the town that deserved the name of art, Clermont had reason to be proud of its intellectual tradition. It numbered four or five hundred students in its college, whose affairs were directed by six regents, along with the principal, " men of property, of upright life, and worthy example." A chair of philosophy had been established by a generous patron, Michel Paschon. M. Savaron, a deputy at the 1614 Estates General, had published in 1607 a very interesting volume on the origins of the town of Clermont. M. de Champflour, a technical adviser at the Cour des Aides, prided himself on being a connoisseur of architecture. The priests of the several religious orders, the canons of the Cathedral, and not a few of the *bourgeoisie* and aristocracy were noted for their wide learning and urbane manners.[22]

Etienne Pascal had a hobby. He was deeply versed in ancient languages and mathematics. As we look back upon the accomplishments of the seventeenth century provincial *bourgeoisie*, we cannot withhold our admiration. They leave us feeling quite humble by comparison! One of the counsellors at the Parliament de Toulouse, for instance, a man named Fermat, whose relationship to the Pascal family will shortly become clear, was one of the great mathematicians of his day. A student of Greek literature, he wrote poetry of his own, and " amused himself " with scientific investigations which were always in his mind during hours of relaxation. It was an age when men were not consumed, as in our day, by a concern to escape from themselves, nor by an incessant feeling of rush and haste. Men in such an age gave themselves to pastimes which served to stimulate the loftiest attainments of the human spirit. They were fully aware of the fact that Time is a somewhat austere personage who respects only that which is carried through in his company. Yet the intellectual activity of a man like Etienne Pascal, seen against the background of his time, must be regarded not only as recreational in inspiration but also as sportive and playful in character.

This would need elaboration because Blaise started out in the same spirit, throwing himself into all that he did, we may well say, as into a game. Then as a result of and in the midst of circumstances we shall try to recapitulate, his disinterested and playful attitude later gave way to a more urgent concern. When, at the age of nineteen, he invented the calculating machine, patiently assembling it piece by piece, it was primarily with a view to helping his father, who used to sit up late into the night over his figures. With the machine at last ready to operate, the pride of Blaise in his achievement inspired something less than modesty in his letters of dedication. In the course of the controversies aroused by his scientific work, his sharp, even biting, style displayed all too well his stubborn determination to be right. His father never failed to stand by him, and to strengthen his spirit of defiance, which in some cases became almost threatening. Little by little his motives were purged and clarified, yielding at last to a single-minded passion for truth, above all else. What passionate minds this Pascal family had!

Etienne believed himself the victim of a pedagogical method of which he could not approve, and thus it was that, after long brooding on the whole matter of education, he had decided to take the training of his children into his own hands. The methods he had chosen to apply seemed to him more reasonable, more direct, and more effective than those he found current in the schools. His main principle was this: "Always hold the child above his task." Keeping this maxim in mind, he taught young Blaise to observe everything with the utmost care, and to reason out the course of his observations at every step, so that he was able to give an account of everything that happened, stage by stage.

Father and son held frequent conversations during the course of each day. These amounted to vital lessons drawn from actual experience, by means of which Etienne filled the receptive mind of young Blaise with a rich store of impressions concerning the thousand-and-one phenomena he met in everyday life. The lad was thus "encouraged in his own instinctive desire to know the reasons and causes of things, and the discipline he received in the habit of rigorous thinking paved the way for decisive experiments later on."[23]

From the observation of physical objects, President Pascal proceeded to a consideration of the use of words, which for Blaise were always inseparable from objects. Through all his life, he felt a natural discontent for empty jargon. Even in boyhood he worked out for himself a rudimentary philosophy of words, which one day was to impel him to inquire into the structure and purpose of grammar. Once fully attained, his sense of the meaning of words was never lost, and this explains the intense vitality of his mature style and the unusual syntax he employed. This is, at least in part, the basis for the comment made by Dr. H. F. Stewart: "No man has written with more magic and mastery of phrase. And this triumph is more than verbal; it is the triumph of a personality: 'Le style c'est l'homme.' Of no one is this more true than of Pascal."[24]

Demand for Truth

The primary purpose of all genuine education is the attainment by each individual of self-direction. In one sense education thus tends to make itself superfluous. This truth gives special point to the remark of St. Cyres concerning Pascal's education: "The boy's best teacher was himself. Very soon he began to notice the little everyday oddities of Nature, and

puzzle over their explanation."[25]   If this same reasoning be
carried a bit further, we should be prepared to defend the seem-
ing paradox that the best teacher is one who trains a student
to be self-taught.   God only knows whether we are justified in
laughing, as we often do, at self-taught men.   Yet Fortunat
Strowski seems to be doing so in the ironical comment:
" Whatever it is that Pascal has to say in his *Pensées*, he
always shouts it aloud like Christopher Columbus discovering
America."[26]   We are inclined to agree, nor would the Pascal
of the *Pensées* question the point : " People are generally better
persuaded by the reasons which they have themselves discovered than by those which have come into the minds of
others."[27]   But Pascal also went on to say : " Let no one say
that I have said nothing new; the arrangement of the subject
is new.   When we play handball, we both play with the same
ball, but one of us places it better.

" I had as soon it were said that I used words employed
before.   And in the same way if the same thoughts in a
different arrangement do not form a different discourse, no
more do the same words in their different arrangements form
different thoughts."[28]

We are able to agree more fully with Fortunat Strowski
when he points out the subtle, penetrating quality of mind
which emerges from the kind of education Blaise received at
the hands of his father : " It encourages the habit of digging
down to the foundation of ideas; it keeps one free from the
association of ready-made notions and conventional patterns of
thought.   It emancipates the mind from those bonds of tradition and social pressure, which make themselves felt as truly
in the intellectual as in the physical world.   All this was
characteristic of Pascal."[29]   This last phrase disposes of the
matter too easily, however, in that it deals only with method,
with the discipline of the mind.

Of greater import is the growth of that *demand for truth*,
which is the fruit of intellectual discipline.   Pascal's elder sister
was well aware of this distinction, which she seeks to make
clear in the biography of her brother Blaise.   She undertakes
to show the relation of method to content : " Thus from his
childhood, he would not yield to anything short of the truth,
as it appeared to him; so that, when no satisfactory explanation
was offered him, he undertook to find it for himself; and when
he became absorbed in such an inquiry, he would not think of

turning from it until he had found an explanation which satisfied him."[30]

Let such a soul feel the touch of the Divine Hand, and we
may guess what inward hunger and thirst were henceforth to
torment him! We may well understand why Pascal's favourite
psalm was to be the long 118th (known to us as the 119th), for
it is essentially a passionate prayer for light and guidance for
man's mind. Pascal knew this psalm by heart, and he used to
repeat its passages, over and over, with increasing intensity:
" Blessed are they that search his testimonies: that seek him
with their whole heart. . . . O! that my ways may be directed
to keep thy justifications. . . . With my whole heart have I
sought after thee: let me not stray. . . . Open thou my eyes.
. . . Make me to understand the way of thy justifications. . . .
Give me understanding, and I will search thy law . . . and
take not thou the word of truth utterly out of my mouth: for
in thy words I have hoped exceedingly. . . . I have thought
on my ways: and turned my feet unto thy testimonies."[31]

Young Blaise was still very far from these spiritual heights
of dedication to God. As yet he was exposed to little more than
the teaching of the Roman Catholic catechism, as were boys of
his age. Coming home from church, he would then study
under his father's guidance. What this home training did for
him, as he started out in life, was to stir deep within a passion
for excellence, that *libido excellendi* in which Blaise later came
to trace, in its most refined form, " that spirit which is contrary
to the spirit of Christianity."[32]

A Basic Distinction

Not that Etienne Pascal was a free-thinker. On the contrary,
he always displayed an attitude of submissiveness and sincere
respect toward religion. He held that an object of faith could
not, by its very nature, be an object of reason, still less subordin-
ated to the dictates of reason. On the other hand, he maintained that faith had no competence whatever in the field of
natural phenomena.

Deeply impressed by the lofty influence of his father, whom
he respected alike for his great wisdom and for the clarity and
force of his reasoning powers, Blaise thus learned from early
childhood to draw a clear line of demarcation between objects
of reason and objects of faith. When the free-thinkers of his
day—in our time we should call them " modernists "—gave

first place to the claims of reason, and undertook to submit everything to rational judgment, Blaise was in a position to detect at once their basic heresy. The distinction taught him so well by his father was deeply rooted in his mind, and it enabled him to exercise untrammelled freedom of thought in the domain of pure science, and yet to retain a childlike spirit of submissiveness in the domain of religion. This does not mean, of course, that he kept his thinking in compartments with respect to different types of subject matter on the same level. It was evident to him that above the level of reason there emerged, at the level of faith, a new *order*, other than the order of nature, and in this sense supernatural.

We may note at this point, in the basic distinction taught him by his father, the first appearance of the three orders of reality : namely, the order of matter, the order of minds, and the order of charity. In this hierarchy, values were to be separated to the point that communication between one and the one immediately above appeared inconceivable. To quote from the famous Fragment 793 of the *Pensées* : " All bodies, the firmament, the stars, the earth and its kingdoms, are not equal in value to the lowest mind; for mind knows all these and itself too; and these bodies know nothing.

" All bodies together, and all minds together, and all their productions, are not equal in value to the least feeling of charity. This is of an order infinitely more exalted.

" From all bodies together, one cannot draw forth one tiny thought; that is impossible, and of another order. From all bodies and minds, one cannot draw forth a feeling of true charity; that is impossible, and of another order, supernatural."[33]

It seems clear that the seed thought of the notion of the three orders lay hidden in the early teaching Blaise Pascal received from his father. We can well imagine Etienne, as he followed his son's questions back step by step in considering some matter that claimed their attention, suddenly stopping with an upraised hand, or lapsing into reverent silence, when they found themselves at the threshold of a question concerning God : " That, my child, is not for us to talk about! " What a reverent spirit it was that moulded the mind of this gifted child, and what fruitful results were to issue from it!

The basic distinction which Etienne Pascal taught his son helped not a little to save Blaise from the scholastic way of thought. His own theology was always " positive theology," or we should say " Biblical theology." It was from the pages of the Bible that Blaise Pascal received the stimulus to search for himself into the secrets of a God who was self-concealed. Etienne Pascal, as we now can see,"[34] prepared the mind of his son for the influence of the Bible.

To sum up : Just as it would be a mistake to suppose that Etienne Pascal was a free-thinker, it would be a mistake to call him a devout man in the ordinary sense. We could not even call him a religious man. His chief interests, in the leisure hours left him after faithfully discharging his public duty, were mathematics and ancient languages. Scientific discussions were exciting to him. We should also remember that he emerged from a Christian tradition which as an *honnête homme* he did not like to discuss in public, however firmly he might hold to it in personal conviction. He paid his formal respects to this tradition, at a safe distance, when occasion required, but it would be too much to say that President Pascal would ever seek out the occasion. Every Sunday without fail he made his way through the tiny passageway leading from his house to the Cathedral. The passageway was in a sense a symbol : it served as a link to keep the oratory in touch with the laboratory.

Etienne was of a stanch, legal temper, rigorous in its concepts of right, taking but slight account of the whims of popular feeling, but finding deep rootage in the soil of Auvergne. This same temper reappeared, in a loftier and purer form, in his son, who was one day to vindicate the Jansenists against the Jesuits in his *Lettres Provinciales*. As it developed, it was enriched by a stream flowing from Christian faith and from the Bible. It came to take full account of the nature of the human soul, and of the scene of humanity in general. The notion held by Blaise Pascal concerning responsibility, together with his concept of human beings as so many distinct personalities, coherent in themselves yet constantly having to suppress elements of corruption, responsible to God and to society—of all this, he was persuaded from having listened as a child to a voice speaking clearly and distinctly of delinquents, accused persons, guilty and condemned criminals, and about the moral law and the law of God. He himself was one day to devote his life to building up cases, when his conscience as a man and as a Christian was laid under constraint !

As to the end product of a long tradition, we can understand

how there came to take shape in Blaise Pascal " the most fully
rounded mind, the best balanced, the most trustworthy in the
realm of the sciences, and at the same time the most restless in
its quest for perfection and for certainty, that France has ever
produced."[35]   A blunt man, full of common sense, a man who
handled things and invented useful devices—the calculating
machine, the barometer, the omnibus—Pascal felt instinctively
that man is a totality, intent first and foremost upon self-
preservation.   His realism was of the utilitarian sort, craving
always for certainty.   It was in this spirit that he read the Bible.
He was not sentimental or mystical in his first approach to the
Bible, but hard-headed, in the manner of one who knew that
there is a rule of life, which can be set down in definite propositions, which must be understood and obeyed.   Man's salvation, after all, is basically a matter of self-preservation.   And if
man is to preserve himself, he dares not dissipate or waste his
efforts.   In Auvergne men never wasted their resources.   A
wise economy starts out from a prudent conduct of everyday
affairs; it continues unbroken in the intellectual economy of a
man of genius, in his search for the inner logic of things, once
he is persuaded basically that God is simple, and that all com-
plexity is a mark of imperfection.   In the case of Blaise Pascal,
his reading of the Bible was a spur to his scholarly inquiry, and
assured him of the reality of the Light behind the curtain.

   This prudent, practical genius always considered himself the
very opposite of a metaphysician.   He always demanded certainty.   There was nothing vague or abstract about the God
he learned to know.   He was the " God of Abraham, of Isaac
and of Jacob," the Living God of the Bible.   For Blaise Pascal
there was no such thing as a substitute or counterfeit; nor could
there be.   Pascal's God was Jesus Christ, God on our earth,
God in history and in our own history.   His final conviction
was to be : We do not know God except through Jesus Christ.

   Starting with all the realistic good sense which he owed to
his native Auvergne, to the common folk and tradesmen of the
Limagne valley, and to a line of men of law in his own family,
Blaise Pascal was prepared to believe " only those accounts of
which the witnesses would die to vindicate their testimony."
He observed that Christianity is primarily a doctrine resting
upon facts, and he came to be devoted to the Bible because it
was presented as a record of facts.   His own Christian faith, in
turn, was to be the faith of a witness, and his argument for

THE EMERGENCE OF A PILGRIM 29

Christianity took the form of a testimony. " He had the spirit of a witness and a martyr; he was prepared to sacrifice even life for his faith, since he had already sacrificed, for the sake of his faith, something to which his heart was far more firmly attached, namely, his prestige, his human pride, science, and even the love of his family."[36]

The author of the *Provinciales* is properly called the creator of French prose primarily because his realism, smacking of the soil, made him the forerunner of Molière's laughter and the " veritable eloquence " of Bossuet. The author of the *Pensées*, while he was concerned with the loftiest inquiries that can occupy the human mind, began a new type of apologetic which abandons every instrument of metaphysics and seizes you, as it were, by the lapel of your coat as a man would do in the street if he were trying to save a careless pedestrian whom he saw in danger. Pascal starts out from your situation and mine. He shows that practical good sense which led the good people of Clermont to plant vegetables in the old moat around their city wall. With every word, his style calls up some image to the mind. Here you see a row of judges, in their ermines and scarlet robes; here a preacher, with a rasping voice and a queer twist to his features, ill-shaven by the barber, and still further besmeared by a chance mishap; here a group of soldiers, drunken brutes in arms with bloated faces, with hands and strength to serve only themselves.

With a sensitive touch Paul Bourget traces the example of Blaise Pascal, as he reflects upon the inequality of our human lot. Speaking of a certain great one, Pascal says : " He has four lackeys, while I have but one. If we settle matters by counting, it is plain that I must give way. By this means we shall find ourselves at peace, which is the greatest of all blessings." Look a bit closely at this last phrase. Bourget writes : " Here you will become fully aware of the transition from physical realism to moral realism. Whatever just and accurate observation Pascal makes concerning even the slightest phenomenon in the material world, he adds an equally precise observation of some psychological truth. Every comment concerning human sentiment which Pascal makes in his *Pensées* is so accurate that it remains true for all time."[37]

A Biblical Horizon

After speaking of the " motionless convulsion " which lends

to Auvergne such a tragic horizon, even during wintry days
when the snow lies like a white cloth over the huge layers of
volcanic rock, leaving one to guess the force of the subterranean
fire and the violence that must have accompanied the eruption,
Bourget ends : " By one of those analogies that defy adequate
expression, the *Pensées* are very much like the Auvergne landscape; the similarity will be noted by one who is fond of
Auvergne and of Pascal.   That he belonged in this respect
to his native province explains . . . the powerful attraction
exerted by this genius, at once so personal in its character,
and yet at the same time so representative of a race, of a whole
region."[38]

These motionless convulsions, which lent a tragic horizon
to Pascal's thought, he found quite as much in the Bible, whose
intimate realism he loved, as in the landscape of Auvergne. He
overheard, in his own heart, a profound echo of the voice of
the prophets. He came to love the rich language of the Book,
pulsing as it did with vitality. He felt at home with Hebrew
notions of the supreme objects of religious devotion, ideas
clothed in flesh and blood, taken from life itself. That is one
reason why he felt that he must make his own translations from
the Bible, and why he often appended an exposition to his own
version, always going to the heart of the experience. That is
in a sense why his theology came to be Biblical, as the wide
gap between the substance of certain doctrines and what the
theologians called their " Scriptural foundations " became so
evident to him.

This man from Clermont had a natural distrust of all
subtlety and circumlocution. It was the substance of things
he must grasp. He went straight to his mark. One of the
ablest critics of literary style, Edouard de Rougemont,[39] made
an analysis not long ago of Pascal's method of writing. It is,
says he, distorted by the excessive speed of composition; he
resorts to frequent abbreviations (this was common, it is true,
at the period when Pascal was writing); words are often
illegible, owing to Pascal's astonishing rapidity of writing.
Threadlike streaks stand in place of whole syllables; at the
same time, it is evident from the coherence of his thought that
there is nothing flighty about his mind. All this notwithstand-
ing, there is still an amazing interval between the swift conception of his thought, and the setting down of the words, however rapidly, on paper. It is rare to find this interval so marked

anywhere, save in the writings of Napoleon or of Beethoven. Reference to such names should remind us, if ever we should be tempted to lose sight of it for an instant, that large place must be given, in any such analysis, to the working of genius.

"What an enigma it is we confront, almost religious in character, whenever a genius appears!" exclaims Maurice Barrès. "How comes it about that the spark gleams in this child, but not in that one, when both are born of the same parents, and under the same sky? How is this point of perfection attained, this perilous equipoise? What shall we make of such an extraordinary blend of saint and sage, of observer and visionary? Pascal rigorously applied the scientific method, but he sensed all the while the reality of supernatural aid. Since we have no other language in which to describe this sublime compounding of qualities, must we then call it a miracle? Was Pascal a black stone that fell from heaven into Clermont on 19 June, 1623? Not at all. Rather was he a block of genuine Auvergne basalt. This noble flame leaped from the same sparks we find in our humblest pebbles." And the writer adds that, if the divine factor in the fashioning of this genius perforce escapes our reckoning, "we may at least understand him in his early actions and his early nurture, until the time when God lifts him, now fully formed, above the level of earthly influences, in order to shape him according to His own design."[40]

This is what we are seeking to accomplish in part, in these opening pages, though we are deeply aware that, in the interplay of these "earthly" influences, the larger part already belongs to God.

II. LIGHT ON AN UPWARD TRAIL

And righteousness shall look down from heaven.

PSALM LXXXV. 11

PASCAL's life appears to have been dominated, in its various periods, by certain distinct principles of conduct.[1] The three major influences upon his thought were: science, the world, and religion. The latter, as it was evident from the beginning, grew in importance to become eventually the dominant, if not indeed the sole, influence on Pascal. His scientific and secular inquiries turned more and more in the direction of religion, until at last they all appeared to converge in his central concern for the Christian faith.

As his mind gave lesser place to worldly concerns,[2] moreover, Pascal's hand held ever more firmly to the Book, to which he always referred as Scripture. Here he found both impulse and insight for " that poem which gathers up the loftiest aspirations of modern man." Thus it is that Maurice Barrès describes what he has called the " Divine Comedy " of the French,[3] namely, the ascension of Blaise Pascal.

The peculiar genius of this personality consists in laying bare the inner logic that lies at the source of human contradictions. When he encounters a network of difficulties, a skein which appears hopelessly tangled, he brings to bear on it the energy of a keen mind, yet always refuses to cut the Gordian knot. Instinctively he feels his way toward a higher plane where the human antinomy is resolved with divine simplicity. His faith thus sharpens his intelligence. *Intelligere* for Pascal is always *intus legere.* As he strains toward a solution, the final stages become easier. It is as though a hand had reached down to help. Has he at last found God, or been found of Him? Does it mean that from the first his wager[4] had been placed on the right side, or that the deciding factor in his choice was, not his own will, but the hand of a " hidden God "? Or, rather, are these not two ways of looking at the same mysterious reality? Thus Pascal confronts the Biblical notion of election, which troubles him, until one day the living Word comes to him: " Console thyself. Thou wouldst not be seeking me, if thou

32

hadst not already found me. . . . Thy conversion, 'tis my concern."[5]

Throughout the course of Blaise Pascal's life and work, there emerged a *unity* of design taking shape amid a diversity of subject matter : geometry, arithmetic, mechanics, physics, theology, polemics, morality, spirituality. The list of the recorded writings of Pascal, as found at the end of Volume 11 of the great Brunschvicg edition we are following, is so encyclopædic in character as to baffle one's imagination. What this list actually indicates, however, is the multiple occasions of a single lifework. Paul Desjardins felicitously describes it when he says that we may here discern in essence " the progressive emancipation of intelligence."[6] Father and son laboured side by side in this undertaking, in one communion of thought, sharing the same environment and marked by the same influences; but from this point on " it was the son who forged ahead and, profiting by the impetus his father had given him, now taught him and in turn led him upward."[7]

A Youthful Prodigy

When Blaise was about seven years old, his father sold his post of Second President of the Cour des Aides to a brother, converted his property into Government bonds, and settled in Paris with his family. From 1631 to the end of 1639 he devoted himself to science and to the education of his children. However, the educational scheme he had decided upon was upset in the case of Blaise. Etienne's opinion was that Latin and Greek should be studied before geometry, which he considered to be the highest form of human knowledge.

At the age of twelve, however, Blaise discovered mathematics by himself, and soon thereafter the youthful prodigy attended the meetings of the Académie Libre with his father. Incidentally the Académie Libre of those days has become the Académie des Sciences of our day. Etienne, overruled, was none the less proud to see his son among such scholars seriously discussing the most difficult questions of mathematics and physics. At sixteen this young genius produced a treatise on conic sections, a work anticipating modern projective geometry.

Etienne Pascal then moved with his family to Rouen in early January, 1640, having been appointed by Richelieu as royal commissioner for taxes in Upper Normandy. There the

Pascals began to make their way in the world. They came to know Corneille. Jacqueline, younger sister of Blaise, at that time won the poet-laureate prize, which was awardèd at the annual competition. It was Corneille himself, impressed as he was by the skill of the poetess, who accepted the award in her name. The following year, Gilberte, Blaise's older sister, was married to her cousin, Florin Périer, who was legal adviser at the Cour des Aides of Clermont. As to Blaise, in his concern about the amount of mechanical work involved in his father's task, he was led, at the age of nineteen, to invent and to construct the first calculating machine.

The Jansenist Quickening

One icy day in January, 1646, Etienne Pascal hurried out on foot to prevent a duel about to take place. He fell on the hard, frozen ground and dislocated his hip. Two pious gentlemen were summoned to attend him—Adrien Deschamps, Sieur de la Bouteillerie, and Jean Deschamps, Sieur des Landes—men who practised medicine and surgery and were also dedicated to good works.

These two brothers were recent converts to Jansenism, an evangelical theology derived from the teachings of Saint Augustine, and adapted to the needs of the seventeenth century by Cornelius Jansen; hence the name of their school, whose centre was Port-Royal. Jean Duvergier de Hauranne, abbé of Saint-Cyran, had been appointed in 1633 confessor of this convent by its Mother Superior, Angélique, one of Antoine Arnauld's daughters. These fundamentalists, exalting the grace of God, had set out to reform Christianity while insisting that personal salvation was possible only in and through the Church of Rome. Conflicts were to be expected; one must note in passing the imprisonment of Saint-Cyran in 1638 and also in 1641 the issue of a papal bull forbidding discussion of questions of grace with special reference to the *Augustinus*. This bulky quarto, a sum of Augustinianism, had only been published in 1640, two years after Jansen's death. Furthermore the substance of the *Augustinus* had been expounded for the general public by Antoine Arnauld in a work on *Frequent Communion* (1643) and this book was immediately the object of passionate debate.

The Pascals were well aware of the storm which spread eventually to the region of Rouen. They were naturally curious to hear all about Jansenism. The Deschamps brothers had quickly won their confidence and respect, and within three months they completely cured Etienne Pascal after the dislocation of his hip.

Morris Bishop pertinently brings out the fact that these men "were in their own persons admirable representatives of the Christian ideal, fulfilling itself in self-abnegation and service to one's fellows. Blaise was of an age to yield readily to hero worship. He was instinctively disposed in favour of the doctrine which had changed their lives, which, they hinted, might change his own."[8] The truth which emerged from that sublime Biblical doctrine, from the very outset, was that man of himself is helpless, and that this helplessness is illustrated by our physical sufferings. Blaise found his own health deteriorating at the time, hence the argument struck him with especial force. He knew from experience how helpless doctors might be—that helplessness which gave Molière material for some of his best scenes: we must not forget that Pascal was living in the middle of the seventeenth century.

The cure the Deschamps brothers were able to achieve being in itself an illustration, Pascal was naturally disposed to follow the teaching of Jansen, who proceeded from concern for bodily suffering to deeper concern over the suffering of the spirit. This all came about, as we have seen, on the plane of personal experience in the Pascal family, at a level familiar alike to father and son. Now, the Bible as experience—or, better, the Bible verified at each step by experience—shows that natural man is not in the state which God originally willed for him: he is a fallen creature. The sin which is rooted in the very core of his being attacks his several faculties, chiefly his will, as the very substance of his being. A vicious circle is thus set in process, by which sin is self-perpetuating, and this vicious circle cannot be broken save by the grace of God. Jansen stands, in this regard, in the line of succession from Saint Paul and Saint Augustine directly. Nothing less than the intervention of divine grace in our lives can free us from helpless mediocrity, from this hidden bondage. Equally true is it in human experience, however, that certain lives are thus regenerated, while others remain in a wretched state in which they appear content. The action of God is the prior fact. It is God's choice which in each case decides. So far, however, from rendering our own energies wholly vain, the grace of God uses them, sustains

them, and repairs their faults and weakness by raising them to
a higher order of being.

It was to an attainment of this state, no less, that Blaise now
aspired.   He was himself attracted to the higher life, before he
sought to attract others.   His youthful ardour was the first to
be quickened by the new doctrine.   Passionate soul that he was,
he at once turned missionary, winning first his " little " sister
Jacqueline, of whom he was particularly fond.   The two of
them appealed to their father, and that lofty soul quietly yielded
to the truth, once he recognized it as such.   " My ideas resist
me," Malebranche was soon to write.   Toward the end of the
year, Gilberte, the elder daughter, who was married now and
had a family of her own, came to Rouen and was won over in
turn, along with M. Périer.   The latter was to lend himself
body and soul to good works all the rest of his life; as for Mme
Périer, she and her children henceforth withdrew from all
gatherings of a social nature, and she herself gave up every sort
of feminine adornment.

The events of our life, as Pascal was one day to say, are
lessons which God Himself has set before us.   In this sense the
accident that befell his father appeared to Blaise, as he looked
back upon it, to be at once the sign and the occasion of God's
purposes for the family.   Is it not clear, from what we know
of Pascal, that he had already felt growing within his mind
" that profound sense of predestination, which gave such a
dramatic quality to his work and to his life " ?[9]

One point needs clarification here, if we are to remove any
trace of misunderstanding which may persist in the minds of
readers familiar with the mistaken phrase, " Pascal's first conversion."   The term *conversion* had a very special meaning in
the seventeenth century; it did not then signify, as it does to-
day, that deep-seated transformation which makes a believer
out of an unbeliever; it meant, rather, especially in Jansenist
wording, " the transition from a more or less dissipated and
worldly life to a life of austere and profound piety."[10]

Let us be even more specific : many writers, when they treat
of Pascal's " first conversion," describe it as primarily intellectual, not to say superficial and transitory, in nature, as
shown by the fact that Pascal soon thereafter " resumed " his
scientific labours.   The truth is that Pascal never interrupted
his scientific studies at all, and that he had no reason to inter-
rupt them, according to the teaching of Saint Augustine, who

greatly influenced his thinking at the time. What was really blameworthy, as he saw it then, was not the study of physics, nor its *employment* in the sincere quest for truth, but the study of science merely for one's own *enjoyment*. To make *enjoyment* the chief end of research was quite evidently to corrupt it, to the degree that it became a sort of greed or lust for learning, a profligate appetite for knowledge, in the form of *libido sciendi*, or even *libido excellendi*. Such a study of science sprang from a prior concern for the self as the centre of things, rather than a concern for seeking out, amid all surrounding natural phenomena, the presence of God and His glory. The very basis, indeed, of this type of intellectual dissipation implied an inversion of the prime principle of eternal Order; it was in essence the *avertio mentis a deo*.[11]

His first contact with Jansenism undoubtedly helped the young scholar, as further evidence will perhaps make clear, to a fuller awareness of this primordial truth. But even at this point it was not really a matter of " conversion "; still less was it so in view of the spiritual heights and depths Blaise was yet to traverse. In the period just following the events we have described, Pascal was as yet far from that mood of complete consecration which marked the closing months of his life.

Confronting the Bible

The Jansenist quickening in the soul of Pascal stirred him to a growing interest in books, which had hitherto played a very limited role in his education. For him, science had been essentially a conversation with nature, needing only the slightest reference to the written word. The problem of religion gave evidence of another Order, quite different from that of experimental science : whereas the latter, under the steady pressure of duly proved facts, sought to free itself—prudently enough, withal—from bondage to ancient tradition, theology was pre-eminently a matter of authority. This distinction, which became more and more clear to Pascal, seems to us to have clarified in Pascal's thinking the distinction between truth dependent upon the oratory and truth dependent on the laboratory. If we examine it more closely, indeed, the new formulation appears as a reshaping of the earlier principle inherited from his father. Once again we find continuity in Pascal's experience.

Now, authority in the field of religion is quite naturally

associated with the authority of certain books, and first of all with the sacred writings. It was thus inevitable that Pascal should be led to confront the Bible. His first significant encounter with the Bible came at a decisive moment in his life. Victor Giraud, who has made a study of Pascal's reading, is persuaded to give first place in importance to the Scriptures, of which Pascal was, as he says, " an assiduous reader," and which he was to know one day almost by heart. Giraud expresses the fervent wish for a book on *Pascal et l'Ecriture*, to stand as companion to the *Bossuet et l'Ecriture* by the Abbé de la Broise. Pascal's reading of the Bible has not been, in his opinion, sufficiently explored: it would shed new light upon " the religious, Biblical, and evangelical tone of the *Pensées*." Special attention, he thinks, should be given to the *Epistles* of Saint Paul, to the writings of Saint Augustine, and to Jansen's *Augustinus*: " There you will find the substance of Pascal's religious thought and of his mysticism."[12]

The doctrinal views of Jansenism accepted by Blaise, at this period, were closely bound up with the Scriptures. This helps further to account for his turning to the Scriptures, by way of Saint Augustine. The Jesuits were following the doctrine of Molina (1535–1600), a Spanish theologian of their religious order, who aimed at a conciliation of human freedom with divine grace and foreknowledge. In this Molinist doctrine Jansen sensed a mortal threat to Catholicism. As he saw it, it was the revival in disguised form of early Pelagianism, which rooted back, through Origen, directly in pagan philosophy. " Seneca had said: To the immortal gods we owe life, to philosophy we owe the good life. According to Jansen, this same human pride, which raised itself against God and even above God, was the very heart of Molinist theology. On the one hand, Jansen was unwilling to concede to the Protestants that God Himself forced man to sin; nor, on the other hand, would he grant to Baïus that there could be sin where there was no free will. To steer between the two rocks, he resolved rigorously to follow Saint Augustine."[13]

The luminous and solid condensation which Brunschvicg gives of the teaching of the *Augustinus*[14] will suffice to indicate the extent to which this work is based upon Holy Scripture, as interpreted by Saint Augustine. " It was from this stream of Christian tradition that Pascal drew inspiration and nourishment, from the time when he first encountered the doctrines associated with the group around Saint-Cyran. Jansen was, in his eyes, the authentic interpreter of Christ."[15] The *Augustinus* was for him the book of true doctrine, the spiritual hearthstone about which his other reading centred. Turning back to Saint Augustine he read, in the original tongue, his letters, his sermons, his essays on *Christian Doctrine* and the *Utility of Believing*, the books against Pelagius, the Commentaries on Scripture. He read the *Discourse on the Reformation of the Inner Man*, which Arnauld d'Andilly had just translated and which the Deschamps brothers had warmly commended to him. Here he found lengthy discourses on the vain desire of knowledge, and on pride, which amply justified the text from Saint John with which the book opens: "All that is in the world is the lust of the flesh, the lust of the eyes, and the pride of life." He read Arnauld's *La Fréquente Communion*, of which four editions were exhausted in six months, and the *Letters* of Saint-Cyran which was also read by his family: "We have here the letter by M. de Saint-Cyran, recently published. . . . We are reading it, and will send it to you soon," wrote Jacqueline and Blaise to their sister Gilberte on April 1, 1648.

But what was the most direct result of all this reading? It was essentially to interest Blaise in making a deeper and more consecutive study of the Bible. From this time on the Scripture held a new meaning for him, which was this: it showed the way to bring about a transformation of heart.[16] It became a rule of life and a means of self-dedication. Mme Périer was doing no more than anticipate the fruits of this Biblical discipline when she wrote: "When he was not yet twenty-four years old, the Providence of God having brought about an occasion which obliged him to read the writings of piety, God illuminated him through this sacred reading in such fashion that he understood perfectly that the Christian Religion obliges us to live for God alone, and to have no object at all other than Himself, and this truth appeared to him as so manifest, so inescapable and so useful, that he terminated all his research: so that from this time on he renounced all other forms of learning in order to devote himself solely to the one thing which Jesus Christ called needful."[17]

The above statement is, of course, too categorical and is controverted by the plain facts, if taken literally: we know that Pascal's scientific activity from then on took its place within a

Christian order, according to the teaching of Saint Augustine and Saint-Cyran on the subject. In whatever he was to do, Pascal always gave first place in his thought to the God of Jesus Christ. The laboratory had become an upper room, and the Bible held the place of honour therein. From this exalted point of view Pascal more and more dominated the human scene as it appeared to him in a fresh perspective. When he intervened in ecclesiastical, scientific, or moral controversies, it was because the sacred cause of truth seemed to him in peril— in the last analysis, the cause of Almighty God; the one thing Jesus Christ has called needful.

Usurpation of Authority Exposed

In October, 1646, soon after he had stirred his family to a renewed concern for Christianity, Pascal watched Pierre Petit, intendant of fortifications, repeat Torricelli's experiment as he had learned it from Mersenne. Finding justification for his new interest, as we have pointed out, in the teaching of Saint Augustine, and Saint-Cyran, Pascal now threw himself into the task of physical research. He was filled, at one and the same time, with enthusiasm for science and with zeal for religion, and he set to work with an energy that was truly staggering. Thus he would clarify those grand syntheses of thought, which were to take shape in the conception of " orders," and in which God was to appear as the principle and the end of all things.

Pascal wished to establish, first of all, the *fact* of the vacuum, by infinite variations upon Torricelli's experiment. Thus he altered the size, length, and shape of the receptacles used, and also the character of the several liquids employed. In the course of this research, he invented the famous syringe which was, in actual fact, the earliest pneumatic device. He set down his conclusions in a pamphlet, which appeared in 1647 under the title *Expériences Nouvelles Touchant le Vide*, remarkable in the acuteness of the observations recorded.

This did not, however, avert a series of attacks upon his scientific report. The sharpest retort came from a Jesuit, Father Noël, teacher and friend of Descartes. Appealing to the *authority* of Descartes in the realm of science, and to that of Aristotle in philosophy, he roundly declared that the notion of a vacuum, synonymous with *nothing*, was inconceivable. In his reply,[18] which was phrased as courteously as the letter from Father Noël had been, Pascal reminded his correspondent of a universal rule which applies to all particular forms of subject matter, whenever the truth is being sought. Here is the formula as Pascal himself gave it : " One should never make a judgment concerning the negative or the affirmative of a proposition, unless that which one affirms or denies have one of the following two conditions : namely, either that it would appear so clearly and so distinctly of itself to the senses and to reason, according as it is subject to the one or to the other, that the mind should have no means of doubting its certainty, and this is what we call a *principle* or an *axiom*."[19] Thus it is that, if equals be added to equals, the sums are equal, which constitutes the first axiom of the First Book of the *Elements* of Euclid. This being understood, Pascal proceeds to the second condition, in the following terms : " Or that it may be deduced as an infallible and necessary consequence of these principles or axioms, upon whose certainty wholly depends that of the consequences which have been derived therefrom; such as this proposition, the three angles of a triangle are equal to the sum of two right angles."[20] This is the famous Proposition XXXII of the First Book, whose demonstration Pascal worked out for himself at the age of twelve.

Unless these specifications are met, so Pascal pointed out in his reply to Father Noël, it could never be more than a matter of *vision*, of *caprice*, of *fantasy*, of *idea*, or at best of *fine thought*.[21] Now, the supposed substance which, on Father Noël's view, was said to fill the vacuum, amounted to one of those arbitrary presuppositions, suspended from unconfirmed facts, which are as difficult to believe as they are to contrive.

Consider for a moment the implications of these hypotheses : For any hypothesis to be true, it is not enough that it should be in harmony with all known phenomena; but if it be contradicted by a single one, it is false. Furthermore, it was of no avail for Father Noël to seek refuge behind definitions, however nominally clear they might be; in order to be valid, a definition must correspond to a reality, and no concept in the mind can take the place of facts, nor claim validity counter to facts.[22] Forewarned against scholastic metaphysics by his reading of the Bible, Pascal was no less forewarned by the habits of experimental science.

He did not in the least confuse what depends upon science with what depends upon religion. Pascal felt that he was on solid ground, for, as we have already pointed out, he carried on his scientific work as a disciple of Saint Augustine and Saint-Cyran. With an inner strength derived from the serenity of his faith, the experimental physicist insisted upon the need for duly established facts, upon having all the facts confirm each hypothesis, and upon adducing facts alone to support the hypothesis.

But there was another side to the question. It concerned a reversal of values which Pascal felt, whether rightly or wrongly, that he must attack; *the very persons who appealed to authority in the field of science were launching a naturalistic, rationalistic method in theology*. To Pascal it appeared that the misunderstanding between Father Noël and himself was twofold; Pascal therefore felt that it was necessary, after restoring to experimental science the naturalistic and rationalistic methods which properly belonged to it, to restore to theology the authority that was its proper due, the sole authority that belongs to it according to the strict teaching of the Scriptures: the authority of the Holy Spirit. He further adds—and it is quite clear from the original manuscript that it is an addition: " We reserve for the mysteries of faith, which the Holy Spirit has itself revealed, that submission of mind which extends our belief to those mysteries which are hidden from sense and from reason."[23]

The controversy with Father Noël thus anticipated the *Provinciales*, in that it showed how fundamental had already become the disagreement between the Biblical thinking of Pascal and the innovating mentality which, as Pascal held, the Jesuits imported into the field of theology. Let it be understood that we are not taking sides as between Pascal and the Jesuits. We are seeking to make Pascal's position clear, and his position is quite evidently exclusive.

This question was already so much on his mind that he developed it at some length in the fragmentary preface to his *Traité du Vide*. In our opinion it is no accident that this fragment appeared at the very time he wrote his first letter to Father Noël.[24] Whenever Pascal was touched to the quick, he became eloquent. The reply to Father Noël was twice as long as the letter itself. Might it not be that the additional note, " We reserve for the mysteries of faith," was expanded into the preface to his treatise?

In this remarkable fragment, Pascal draws a very sharp line of demarcation between matters in which one seeks only to

know what others have set down, as in the case par excellence
in theology, and those matters which are subject to sense and
to reason.   In the former case we must have recourse to books,
by whose authority alone we may seek for more light.   In
them, authority is inseparable from truth, and we cannot know
the truth save by this authority : " . . . so that to lend full
certainty to those matters which are incomprehensible to reason,
it suffices to point to where they are found in the sacred books
(just as, in order to demonstrate the uncertainty of those most
likely things, it is enough to show that they are not therein
contained); because its principles are superior to nature and to
reason, and, the mind of man being too feeble to attain them
by its own efforts, it cannot reach up to those lofty thoughts,
unless it is sustained by a strength which is all-powerful and
supernatural."   Here we find a clearer formulation of the
notion of " orders," which was to become the keystone of the
arch of the Pascalian edifice.   The first hint of it, let us remember, we found in the symbol of oratory and laboratory.
What was still required, before it should take shape in Pascal's
clear and mature consciousness, was a still more vital contact
with the Word of God.   It was the Scriptures which gave to
Pascal's thought the impulse that was to carry it to its zenith.

In matters which are subject to science and to reason and in
which only the natural habit of our thinking is involved, so
the preface continues, " authority is useless; reason alone has
grounds for such knowledge."   In the question of competence
at this level, Pascal is quite categorical in his affirmation.   He
speaks with the tone of the jurist, as he had learned it from his
father, President Pascal.

Two conclusions were to be quite rigorously deduced from
this affirmation : on the one hand, we must " complain of the
blindness of those who appeal to authority alone for proof in
physical matters, rather than to reasoning or to experiments ";
but, on the other hand, we should be overcome with *veritable
horror* at " the malice of others, who look to reason alone in
theology, rather than to Scripture and to the Fathers."   There,
indeed, lay the sovereign authority for Pascal in theology : in
the Scripture interpreted according to the Tradition.   Should
anyone dare to touch that, it was sure to arouse a holy indigna-
tion in his passionate soul.   Whereas those persons " who do
not dare to contrive anything new in physics " are only " timid
fellows," whose courage needs to be braced up, it was needful,

on the other hand, " to confound the insolence of those rash persons who undertake to launch novelties in theology." It is clear that the *Provinciales* were already within the perspective of his thinking when he wrote the preface to the *Traité du Vide*. When Arnauld was to appeal to Pascal, in January, 1656, to be spokesman for Port-Royal against the Jesuits, Blaise had only to give free expression to his profoundest conviction, already of long standing, and it was as the champion of Scripture and of Tradition that he was to enter the lists on behalf of a cause long recognized by him as sacred. Whether his stand, in that instance, was well or poorly taken, his quarrel with the Jesuits was fundamental in nature. In this respect there was never any deviation from the main pathway of Pascal's thought and line of duty. But let us return to the physicist facing his Bible!

To carry on scientific research in the spirit of Saint Augustine and Saint-Cyran was to prove in the long run a more delicate undertaking than he had at first believed. A threefold concupiscence beset him at every step of the way. His Bible told him that it were expedient for him that one of his limbs should wither, rather than that his whole body should " be cast into hell."[25] The physicist confronting his Bible was not yet, however, resigned to such mutilation. An even wider range of experience—the experience of the world—must be his before he would agree to this radical operation. But by then the operation would have to be all the more radical because of the long delay upon which this passionate soul had insisted before yielding his consent. And then, by a stroke of irony which tells us a good deal about the misery of our human situation, when he finally did surrender, it was in response to that very *libido excellendi* which had always pressed upon him and which carried its own stumbling-block within itself.

When Paul Valéry writes that " this French Hamlet of Jansenist persuasion "[26] " has exaggerated, frightfully and crudely, the opposition of knowledge and salvation,"[27] he does something less than justice to the immense effort of goodwill with which Pascal entered on that pathway in which there are so many pitfalls—pitfalls which Paul Valéry, as it happens, does not believe even exist.

Pitfalls in the Pathway

In the summer of 1647, Blaise and his younger sister

Jacqueline, moved back to Paris. Blaise's health, which had
been poor for a long time, took a turn for the worse. He
was exhausted by the bleedings and purgings ordered by his
physicians.

Upon their arrival in Paris, Blaise and Jacqueline came into
closer contact with the Jansenists, especially with Monsieur
Singlin, who was a great preacher and an experienced spiritual
adviser. Jacqueline was soon won over by the Port-Royalists,
and was subsequently convinced that she could become a nun
" reasonably " in their community. From then on, her increasing desire for such a vocation was ever present. The
experience of a closer contact with Port-Royal did not turn
out to be such a happy one for her brother, however.

In conversations with Monsieur de Rebours, the assistant of
Monsieur Singlin, Pascal had suggested the possibility of preparing " the way of the Lord " by a preliminary demonstration
based on science and reasoning—a first hint apparently of the
vindication of Christianity to which he intended to devote the
latter part of his life. As yet, however, he had not entirely
clarified his ideas on the subject and some of the statements he
made were considered by Monsieur de Rebours as being but
the expression of an alarming spiritual pride. The more Pascal
tried to clear up the situation, the more reticent the Jansenist
confessor became. The misunderstanding between the two
men resulted only in unsolved and irreconcilable points of view.

In 1648, Etienne Pascal resigned his position in Rouen and
moved with his family to Paris, where he expected to spend
the rest of his life peacefully with his children. The news of
Jacqueline's religious vocation, however, distressed him. He
opposed it and was prone to be suspicious of both brother and
sister, who he saw were in league together. His anger died
down, however, when Jacqueline promised him that she would
not retire from the world during his lifetime. His death took
place in 1651 and then she felt free to answer the call to become
the " bride of Christ."

Jacqueline entered Port-Royal early in January, 1652, and,
having taken her final vows, in June of the same year became
Sister Sainte-Euphémie.

In the meantime her lonely brother had made new friends,
namely, Miton, the Chevalier Méré, and the Duke de Roannez.
As the guest of the Duke, Pascal travelled with them to the
Province of Poitou of which his ducal friend was the Governor.

Chronology at this point remains uncertain, but it seems plausible to state that the above-mentioned journey took place during the spring of 1653. Thus Pascal's " worldly period," which in this brief survey we cannot pause to consider, lasted in all probability a little more than a year. It is likely that it opened in connection with the money settlements involved in the inheritance of Etienne Pascal and the subsequent religious profession of Jacqueline and closed at the end of the year 1653. It was then, according to Mme Périer, that her brother was overcome by " a great disgust with the world."

During the greater part of 1654, the mood of his day-by-day life came to be one of " quiet desperation."[28] He was baffled by the paradox of human nature, a paradox which philosophers usually recognize but somehow never resolve. Man is such an obvious mass of contradictions : a monster and a prodigy, "judge of all things and a. helpless earthworm, depository of truth and sink of uncertainty, crown and scum of created things."[29] Among philosophers, the Stoics single out man's nobility, while the sceptics see only his baser side. Pascal came to realize that neither Epictetus nor Montaigne is right : " Man is neither angel nor brute, and the untoward thing is that he who would act the angel acts the brute."[30] It would be dangerous indeed to place undue stress on either side of man's nature, leaving him in ignorance of the other : " Man must not be led to believe that he is on the level either with the brutes or with the angels. . . . He must know the one and the other."[31] Does this mean that, since the truth lies somewhere between Epictetus and Montaigne, there might evolve a philosophy that should combine the merits of both? Pascal carefully considered the prospect, but concluded that such eclecticism would be bound to fail, since the teachings of the two schools of thought would end by destroying one another : " One school considering nature as incorruptible, the other as irretrievable, they could not escape either pride or sloth, the two sources of all vice; since they can only abandon themselves to vice through cowardice, or escape it by pride. While some knew the excellence of man, they were unaware of his corruption, so that they easily avoided sloth, but lost themselves in haughtiness. While others recognized the infirmity of nature, they were unaware of its dignity. Therefore they were easily able to avoid vanity, but fell into despair."[32]

Despair. This word now characterized the mood of Blaise

Pascal. His short venture in the world of men and affairs had led him to a state of spiritual aridity in which he found himself deprived of communion with God.

His distress seemed to him all the greater as he compared it with the bliss of Jacqueline. In September, 1654, he came to the point of confessing to her his aversion for the beguilements of the world, his continual sorrow at being so " greatly abandoned " of God that actually he no longer felt any attraction to Him. Looking back at his past Christian experience, he was now in a position to differentiate between the inner urge of divine grace and the useless efforts of his own mind to find God. Jacqueline could only advise him to rely upon the ways of repentance.

Light on the Book

Alone in the darkness of his soul, Blaise turned to his Bible. He opened it at the beginning of the seventeenth chapter of The Gospel According to John, where Jesus is shown preparing Himself for His sacrifice on the cross. Having given up all inclination to struggle or the slightest pretence to a power he might call his own, and at the same time infinitely weary, Blaise groped for Jesus in order to watch with Him. And all of a sudden, during the night of November 23, 1654, Blaise's room was flooded with the very Light of the flaming bush that burned and did not burn out. A divine message came to him, which he feverishly scribbled down on a slip of paper. He afterward copied, with a few variations, the text of this revelation on a parchment. Both documents were discovered only after his death, sewn into the lining of his coat. This record allows us to follow Pascal's mystical illumination. It testifies to the fact that the written Word of the Book and the living Word are one and the same Word. It shows that God speaks to His people in and through the Bible, often by illuminating such and such a verse for the seeker. It vindicates the ways of repentance and calls for nothing short of total surrender. Above all, it exalts the Christ. A throbbing undertone of joy animates this message of election.

Let us now give the text of the moving document.

In the year of Grace, 1654,
On Monday, 23rd of November, Feast of St. Clement, Pope and Martyr, and of others in the Martyrology,

Vigil of Saint Chrysogonus, Martyr, and others,
From about half-past ten in the evening until about half-past twelve

FIRE

God of Abraham, God of Isaac, God of Jacob, not of the philosophers and scholars.
Certitude. Certitude. Feeling. Joy. Peace.
God of Jesus Christ.
My God and thy God. .
" Thy God shall be my God."
Forgetfulness of the world and of everything, except God.
He is to be found only by the ways taught in the Gospel.
Greatness of the soul of man.
" Righteous Father, the world hath not known Thee, but I have known Thee."
Joy, joy, joy, tears of joy.
I have fallen away from Him.
They have forsaken Me, the Fountain of living waters.
" My God, wilt Thou forsake me? "
May I not fall from Him for ever.
" This is life eternal, that they might know Thee, The only true God, and Jesus Christ, Whom Thou hast sent."
Jesus Christ.
Jesus Christ.
I have fallen away: I have fled from Him, denied Him, crucified Him.
May I not fall from Him for ever.
We keep hold of Him only by the ways taught in the Gospel.
Renunciation, total and sweet.
Total submission to Jesus Christ and to my director.
Eternally in joy for a day's exercise on earth.
I will not forget Thy word. Amen.[33]

Blaise Pascal lived up to this last resolution. A humble penitent, overcome by distrust and contempt of self, his sole desire from then on was to be counted for naught in the esteem and memory of man. He would never again sign his writings with his own name, or even have his name mentioned, and as he left Paris he secretly assumed that of Monsieur de Mons. He retired first to Vaumurier, then dwelt among the solitary souls of Port-Royal. In fact he might have lived there for the rest of his days, had not his friends the Jansenists called on him to vindicate their cause in their controversy with the Jesuits. But even then, partly for the sake of his own safety, it is true, he would sign his *Lettres Provinciales* with the name of Louis de Montalte.

New Insights

As he resumed his meditations at Port-Royal of the Fields among the solitary souls he was driven to a new insight of man's basic problems. It appeared to him then that their solution was indeed beyond the reach of human wisdom, but that at the same time man was not left to his own resources : " Whence it appears that God wishing to solve the difficulty of our being unintelligible to ourselves, has concealed the knot so high, or we might better say so low, that we are indeed unable to reach it; so that it is not by the proud exercise of reason, but rather by the simple submission of reason that we can truly know ourselves."[34] Christian teaching indeed held the key to the whole matter : " There are two truths of faith equally certain : one, that man in the state of creation or of grace is raised above all nature, rendered like unto God and sharing in His divinity; the other, that in the state of corruption and sin man is fallen from this state and made like unto the beasts."[35] Pascal supported both propositions by direct reference to Scripture, citing on the one hand such passages as : " I will pour out my spirit upon all flesh,"[36] and, on the other hand, statements which compare man to senseless beasts : " I said in my heart concerning the sons of men [that God would prove them, and shew them to be like beasts]."[37] It is therefore profoundly true that the Christian religion " so justly tempers fear with hope, through that double capacity of grace and sin common to all, that it makes one infinitely more humble than reason alone can do, but without causing despair; and exalts one infinitely more than does the pride of nature, yet without arrogance."[38] Well can we understand, then, the eager enthusiasm of Pascal's conclusion : " The Christian religion alone has been able to cure these twin vices, pride and sloth, not expelling one by means of the other, according to the wisdom of the world, by expelling both according to the simplicity of the Gospel."[39]

The simplicity of the Gospel ! It was the *simplicity* of the Gospel, that is to say its directness and purity, which seemed to

Pascal to be as a hidden knot, beyond the reach of ordinary reason, which left apparently insoluble the riddle of human existence. More and more Pascal found his answers suggested by the insights of the Bible.

If we may believe the somewhat biased account of his elder sister, Pascal came at last to the point when he devoted to prayer and Scripture-reading all the time that was not given to charitable enterprises : " One should add that the two occupations were not distinct for him, since he meditated on Scripture while praying. He used to say that study of the Scripture was a science, not of the mind, but of the heart, that it was intelligible only to the upright in heart and that all others found naught but obscurity in it, that the veil which lay on Scripture for the Jews was also there for bad Christians, and that charity was not only the object of Scripture but the door to it. He went on further to say that one was well minded to understand Holy Writ when one hated himself and enjoyed dying unto Christ. It was in this state of mind that Pascal read the Holy Scripture, and he so persevered in this that he knew nearly all the Bible by heart. If someone misquoted it in his presence, he would declare firmly, ' That is not from Scripture,' and would point to the precise place whence it came. He knew all that could help him to attain a perfect understanding of the truth, whether of faith or of morality."[40]

The account given in 1684 is even more explicit : " He read all the commentaries with great care, since his respect for religion, bred in him from the time of his youth, had now turned into an ardent love, a love sensitive to all the truths of faith, whether concerning submission of the mind, or concerning the practice of morality in which all religion issues, and this love led him to labour unceasingly to overcome everything that was opposed to these truths."[41]   Lhermet only paraphrases the above statements when he declares that for Pascal the Bible was the source of all supernatural truth and the foundation of the moral life; that Pascal spent the best hours of each day in Scriptural study and meditation; and that he devoted all his strength and health to stanchly defending the Bible and planting it in the hearts of men. It is virtually impossible, he adds, to understand Pascal without taking into account the Biblical atmosphere in which he lived.[42] As a matter of fact, Pascal is unfathomable apart from the Bible. " The inspiration of the Bible runs through the whole of his work."[43]   Of all the influ-

ences which moulded his thought, the greatest was the Holy
Scripture.

Inner Conflicts

As we have already realized, Pascal never treated the Bible
as an isolated document. He read it in the full light of the
long tradition of the early Fathers, the Councils, and the Popes.
Blaise Pascal, be it remembered, lived and died a fervent
Roman Catholic. He considered himself the standard-bearer
of the Catholic and Apostolic Church, and he sought to make
this clear especially when he took up the cause of the Port-
Royalists in their controversy with the Jesuits. The writer of
the *Provinciales* was resolutely opposed to every form of heresy.
His unbroken allegiance to the Church of Rome was a matter
on which he would tolerate no compromise. Moreover expediency was foreign to him. The unyielding rigour of his
Christian conscience was shown especially on one occasion
when he actually fainted at the suggestion that his friends at
Port-Royal were willing to compromise on what he held to be
a vital matter of faith. He later explained to his sister Gilberte
that his fainting had been due to the intensity of his feeling :
" When I saw all those very persons waver and succumb who
should have been the defenders of the truth, and to whom I
believed God had made the truth known, I confess that I was
so overcome with grief that I could not endure it, and so col-
lapsed."[44] The whole incident is fully consistent with all that
we know of Pascal's character[45]—the type of character that
only the Bible can mould.

Pascal was indeed a Roman Catholic. There was nothing
he dreaded more than the thought of being separated from the
Mother Church. And yet his position within the Church came
to be regarded as bordering narrowly on heresy. His Port-
Royal friends, whose position he shared, likewise insisted in
vain that they were fully loyal to Rome. This peculiar situation should be borne in mind when we read Gazier's statement
that Jansenism was a phantom and a monster, whose sinister
character was understood only by the Jesuits and their
followers.[46] The Jansenists have been called the Puritans of
the Roman Church. They were earnest students of the Bible,
and held to a strict interpretation of its teaching in the life of
the mind as well as in daily conduct. Affiliation with such a
group on the part of an individualistic genius like Pascal, while

he was at the same time retaining a sincere loyalty to the
Church, inevitably led to inner conflicts, which were all the
more intense because his faith was vindicated by a personal
experience of God.   There were times when the inner strain
grew to the point of producing a divided personality in a Christian layman who prayed and lived the Book.

It is tempting to ask whether the acuteness of Pascal's
" anguish," as it has been called, is not to be traced to this
tension within his own soul.   When, for example, he was
drafting the eighteenth *Provinciale*, addressed to the Com-
mander of the Jesuit Order in France, Father Annat, who was
also the King's confessor, a poignant cry was wrung from him :
" If my letters are condemned in Rome, that which I condemn
in them is condemned in Heaven. *Ad tuum, Domine Jesu,
tribunal appello.*"[47]   Now, Letter XVIII was written at the
very moment when the *Provinciales* were about to be placed
on the Index.   It took the form of an answer to the charge of
heresy brought against the opponents of the Jesuits.   Pascal's
cry may have been, as Jovy suggests, no more than an echo of
Saint Bernard's appeal for absolute justice, to which as a Christian he also aspired.[48]   Steeped as he was, however, in the
writings of Montaigne, Pascal had a way of so assimilating
what he read as to make the substance of it his own.   Jovy
admits to some doubt as to precisely what Pascal implied by the
Latin quotation in question.[49]   Henri Bremond takes it to re-
flect at most a passing rebellious impulse.[50]   Yet we learn that
in the year 1679, when the persecution of Port-Royal was resumed, Mother Angélique placed in the folded hands of a
deceased nun a written request to the Great Shepherd of the
sheep, the request beginning with a phrase strikingly similar
to the words of Pascal and Saint Bernard : " We appeal to Thy
tribunal, Lord Jesus."[51]   Pascal, like the Port-Royal nuns, was
carrying his appeal to the Supreme Judge of all judges.   It was
the plea of a man who, through his profound study of the Bible,
had come to know God's will in all its directness, and was now
taking his stand upon the basis of that knowledge.

The sense of direct awareness of the will of God is indeed
the fruit of a close study of the Scripture.   President John A.
Mackay has made this suggestive comment on the verse from
Psalm 85 which reads, *Truth shall spring out of the earth,
and righteousness shall look down from heaven* : " Truth is
represented as being of the earth, something that springs up

from beneath to apprehend that which comes down from above. But as righteousness means the secret of right relations between God and man, and between man and man, it can never be adequately apprehended as an idea. To be known it must be intensely desired and submitted to."[52] Here is the true interpretation of Pascal's appeal to the divine tribunal. Well it might stand as a motto for the whole of our inquiry. It summarizes quite clearly the basic fact that has emerged from our study, namely, that Pascal's growing faith issued in an ever keener intelligence, the kind of intelligence which led him to detect and grasp the inner logic lying at the heart of human contradictions. It was no mere curiosity that drove Pascal forth upon his quest. His mature life began with a concern which was profoundly religious in character and in scope; it ended in utter commitment to Jesus Christ.

Utter Consecration

In his commitment, the thinker was inseparable from the mystic and the saint. Not only did his thought centre around the Christ, but as he prayed and lived his Bible, he came to an organic contact with the Man in the Book. Uplifted into heights unknown to mortal man, he came to partake of the agony of his Lord with such fervent love that he actually heard the crucified Saviour say to him :

" I was thinking of thee in My agony; I have shed such and such drops of blood for thee. . . .

"'I am more of a friend to thee than such a one and such a one, for I have done more for thee than they and they would not suffer what I have suffered for thee and they would not die for thee at the time of thy infidelities and cruelties, as I have done."

The moving dialogue reached a climax of grandeur as Jesus brought from Blaise these words of utter consecration, " Lord, I give Thee all."[53]

Upon reaching such heights of the *Mystère de Jésus*, we would not draw nigh, for the place whereon we stand is holy ground.

Let us simply say that every Christian should pause on Good Friday to read the few pages of the *Mystère* and then keep all these things and ponder them in his heart. For, in the words of Blaise Pascal, " Jesus will be in agony until the end of the world; we must not sleep during all that time."[54]

III. "A LAMP UNTO MY FEET"

Thy word is a lamp unto my feet, and light unto my path.

"It is written . . . and it is written. . . . And this is why Jesus Christ, who said . . . also said . . . But he did not say . . ." Pascal's thinking in his latter years might well have been summarized in these five Scriptural propositions, based upon five Biblical texts,[1] forming a solid framework of eight lines in Fragment 949 of the *Pensées*.[2] Alike in his life and in his work, the Bible came to hold such an important place for Pascal that, if we wish to establish the chronology of some un-dated writings of his on a moral or spiritual theme, the surest criterion would be to rely upon the number and character of Biblical quotations or allusions found therein. Whether he was summarizing his position during a controversy, or establishing the proper ground for some personal maxim, or giving counsel as a Christian layman, Pascal came to rely more and more upon the Bible.

Biblical Radicalism

"Anyone who seeks to give meaning to Scripture, without taking it directly from Scripture, is a foe to Scripture." This principle indicates clearly enough the Biblical radicalism of one who had heard Christ Himself say to him: " I am present with thee by My Word in Scripture."[3] For Pascal, "all depends upon the blessing of God, to be attributed only to things done for Him, according to His rules and His ways, the manner being thus as important as the thing itself, and perhaps more."[4] To hold fast to Scripture interpreted according to Scripture, was to hold fast alike to the commands of God and to the ways He taught to the man of faith, the man who had prayed to Him, pouring out his heart in the words of Psalm 118: " Make me to understand the way of thy justification."[5] This man of faith had already come to acknowledge in the words of this same psalm: " By what does a young man correct his ways? By observing thy words."[6] And he had learned that we do not

* Psalm cxix, numbered cxviii in the Douay Bible, was Pascal's favourite.

know these ways save through Jesus Christ, that " we know
God by Jesus Christ alone," that " we know ourselves only
through Jesus Christ "; we know life and death only through
Jesus Christ," and that " the Scripture has Jesus Christ alone
for its object."[7] It is Jesus Christ who, in this double capacity,
gives meaning to Scripture, as the object of Scripture and as
being present in Scripture. That is why anyone wishing to
interpret the meaning of Scripture must take it from the Scripture. This came to be the maxim guiding a man whose
philosophy was henceforward Christ-centred, a Christian who
learned to recognize in the Bible the same voice he heard speaking to him in his prayers, and who from now on came to pray
through his Bible even more.than to read in it. After the
manner of the brethren in the book of The Acts,[8] he was found
" daily searching the Scriptures, whether these things were
so."[9]

We have not adequately stressed, writes Robert Vallery-
Radot,[10] the continued contact, on Pascal's part, with the Bible,
and with Saint Augustine, and most of all with Saint Paul.
This same writer goes on to indicate, as we have done, that
Pascal's devotion to the Bible was inseparable from his love of
Christ, which shone forth in his sublime countenance, and thus
revealed the central secret of Pascal's genius.

The Supreme Reference

Every scholar who has made a study of Pascal's reading
agrees that the very first importance must be given to the Holy
Scriptures.[11] This preponderant place was apparently given to
the Bible, especially after the famous night of November 23,
1654, not only as a result of the special revelation attested by
the *Mémorial*, but also from the fact that, after this experience,
Pascal lived in close contact with Port-Royal, where the Bible
was held in great respect. Pascal was present at the Vaumurier
meetings which established the text of the Mons edition of the
New Testament. He followed closely the discussions of this
whole matter among the Jansenist theologians. He explored
the Port-Royal library at length, finding it particularly well
stored in editions of the Bible, and in works relating to the
Bible.

When he found himself engaged in full-fledged controversy
with the Jesuits, the author of the *Provinciales* turned constantly to the Bible for reference and for guidance. Thus in

the first *Provinciale* he examined Arnauld's assertion according to which grace had failed Peter when he denied his Lord. Fragment 744 of the *Pensées*[12] shows Pascal turning to the Bible for an explanation of Peter's behaviour. Domat scrutinized the same Biblical texts here adduced to by his friend Blaise.[13] It is not possible in the present survey to pause on the controversy between Jesuits and Jansenists and to bring out the tremendous part played by Scripture in the *Provinciales* and other polemical writings. We hope to devote entire chapters to this all-important subject in a future book on Pascal. Likewise a study of the *Pensées* will show the polemist absorbed in the consultation of Scripture as he was drafting his letters and facta.

Pascal had turned from experimental science to the Bible as his teacher. The only truth that henceforth mattered greatly to him, he found set forth in the texts of revelation which gave him answers to his questions: " He applied all his energy to the interpretation of these texts, becoming a disciple, not only of the Hebrew writers who edited the Old Testament, but also of the Jewish rabbis who had disclosed and established its figurative meaning. Pascal was loyal to the tradition of Saint Paul and to the spirit of Jansen, who unceasingly condemned the corrupting influence of Origen and the Scholastics, and sought to purify religion of all traces of Platonic metaphysics and Stoic ethics, that is to say, of all pagan influences. Pascal sought to rediscover Christianity in its original form, distinguishing it clearly from its late contact with the mentality of the West, and welding it solidly to the Judaism which was its prime source."[14]

In this regard Pascal developed the very thesis which, in the years 1847 to 1850, Kierkegaard was to take up with new vigour, and to press to its logical ultimate consequences. In his *Comparaison des Chrétiens des Premiers Temps avec ceux d'Aujourd'hui* Pascal pointed the way for the author of *The Sickness Unto Death* (1849), of *Training in Christianity* (1850) and of the bellicose pamphlet *The Moment* (1853). Both men made quite clear the incompatibility between the spirit which inspired Christianity in its beginnings and its condition in modern times. " This antagonism dates from the day when the Church undertook to enter into intimate relations with ' the world,' with ' this age,' that is to say, with culture as resting upon purely human foundations."[15] It was to find its most vehement expression in Kierkegaard's pained outcry: "The Christianity of the New Testament no longer exists! "[16] The identical protest, in Pascal as in Kierkegaard, roots in a similar evangelical consciousness, whose theme is well stated in the title of one of Kierkegaard's *Edifying Addresses: Purity of Heart Is to Will One Thing*.[17]

In his later years Pascal came to acknowledge " that there is one substantial truth, and that that alone is the truth."[18] For him, faith was knowledge in the full sense of the term, " above sense and reason, but not contrary to them."[19] What determined the true nature òf faith, for Pascal, was Scripture. We may note an edifying analogy on this point, between Pascal and Saint Paul.[20] Faith is what reveals to us ourselves, and reveals other men to us for what they are. All genuine psychology finds its starting-point in " the most ancient book in the world and the most authentic."[21] All history appears as sacred history, once it is seen in the perspective of this Book. Pascal said in his own way, before Bossuet, that man frets, but God leads him.

Indeed Pascal is the forerunner of Bossuet's thinking as evidenced in the *Discours sur l'Histoire Universelle* (1681) and in the *Politique Tirée de l'Ecriture Sainte* (publ. 1709). How glorious it was for Pascal ." to see with the eyes of faith the history of Herod and of Cæsar "![22] " How fine it is to see, with the eyes of faith, Darius and Cyrus, Alexander, the Romans, Pompey, and Herod working, without knowing it, for the glory of the Gospel! "[23] Faith, by giving us a true understanding of prophecy, draws back the curtain and shows history as a single drama with a unifying theme. The Messiah appeared at the time " foretold by the state of the Jewish people, by the state of the heathen, by the state of the temple, by the number of years."[24] What a wonderful thing! When a human intelligence is enlightened from above, it can trace the conflict of God's purposes at grips with the purposes of man, and watch man's purposes take their proper place at last palpitating within the purpose of God! Is it true that neither Josephus nor Tacitus, nor other historians, spoke of Jesus Christ? " So far is this from telling against Christianity, that on the contrary it speaks for it."[25] The fact is that " if Jesus Christ had come just to sanctify, all Scripture and all things would tend to that end, and it would be quite easy to convince unbelievers. If Jesus Christ had only come to blind, all His conduct would confuse; and we would have no means of convincing unbelievers." As it was, in the words of Isaiah,[26] Jesus Christ would rise *in sanctificationem et in scandalum*.[27]

Pascal frankly faced the contradictions found in Scripture and submitted to them, being convinced that the source of all heresy is the exclusion of one truth on behalf of another.[28] In Fragment 776, for example, he cites Biblical texts which declare in substance: " Fear not, provided you fear; but if you fear not, then fear."[29] The statements appear to be mutually exclusive. But Pascal, facing the situation candidly, sets forth the following principle: " To understand Scripture, we must have a meaning in which all the contrary passages are reconciled."[30] To understand Pascal would be to discover just this meaning in his work,[31] particularly in the work of his later years. A detailed analysis of Section XI of the *Pensées* from this point of view would be fruitful and instructive. The *Abrégé de la Vie de Jésus-Christ*[32] stands, in our judgment, as the culmination of this effort at clarification, in the light of Pascal's conviction that " in Jesus Christ all the contradictions are reconciled."[33]

It is Jesus Christ, in the final analysis, who gives Scripture its authenticity and its meaning. In Pascal's eyes, however, this authenticity was evident from one end of Scripture to the other. Moses was contemporary with the events he described in this sense that he was brought quite close to these events by the small number of generations that separated him from them,[34] whereas " truth is perverted only by the change of men."[35] Shem, who saw Lamech, who saw Adam, saw also Jacob, who saw those who saw Moses; " therefore the deluge and the creation are true."[36] In this connection, Pascal opposes the sacred writers to " those fabulous historians " who " are not contemporaneous with the facts about which they write."[37] Furthermore the sincerity of the Jews is beyond question, and this lends added distinction to the contrast between sacred and profane writers: Moses does not hide his own shame, whereas Josephus hides the shame of his nation.[38] Isaiah declares: " This book shall be for a testimony,"[39] and we must admit this truly extraordinary fact, that the Jews lovingly preserve a book which denounces them.[40]

O fathomless wisdom of the hidden God! The Jews never understood how it was that God, in carrying out His profound plan, was able to veil the entire life of Christ and of Christianity

within the depths of the Hebrew text. The Jews saw in the
text only the carnal meaning which suited them, and it was
this which actually saved the Scriptures for us. Why was The
Book of Ruth preserved? Why the story of Tamar?[41]
Everything in the Bible is there for a reason. The more Pascal
examined these various books, scattered through the centuries
and later miraculously gathered together, the more truths he
found in them, the more he found this succession, this religion,
divine. The more he admired it in its authority, its duration,
its perpetuity, its morality, its conduct, its doctrine, its effects,
the more frightful he found the darkness that was foretold for
the Jews. And it was with unspeakable exultation that he held
out his arms to a Redeemer, foretold for four thousand years,
who had come to suffer and to die for him, Blaise Pascal, on
earth, at the time and under all the circumstances foretold.[42]

There are clearly two meanings, therefore, in Scripture : the
literal, or carnal, meaning and the spiritual meaning. Pascal
then proceeds to suggest this principle of interpretation :
" When the word of God, which is really true, is false literally,
it is true spiritually."[43] Are there numerous statements and
expressions which shock our human way of seeing and speaking? It is because they must be spiritually understood. Such,
for example, as these : " God is jealous "; " He accepts the
odour of our sweet-smelling savour "; et cetera. The Old
Testament is a type,[44] Pascal tells us. The Jews were not able
to read it aright because they were carnal; and thus it came
about that they misunderstood Jesus in His greatness as foretold; for they sought in Him merely carnal greatness.[45] No
man can attain to the full meaning of Scripture save by charity,
inasmuch as charity is the unique object of Scripture. Everything in Scripture is figurative, save that which leads to charity.

At this point, however, Pascal would guard against over-
statement. There is danger that either of two errors may
arise out of what has just been said : The first consists in
taking everything literally; the second, in taking everything
" spiritually."[46] Pascal consequently promises that he will
" speak against excessively figurative language "[47] and " far-
fetched " figures of speech.[48] He denounces the " extrava-
gances of the Apocalyptics, Preadamites, Millenarians, etc."[49]
We are at a loss, in fact, to know wherein lies our great admiration for this passionate soul, henceforth so completely devoted
to the Bible : whether for his enthusiasm or for his firm

moderation. Let no one think of Pascal as a romanticist : even in his most enraptured moods, he still remains a classicist—indeed, one of the most eminent craftsmen of French classicism.

A classicist in spirit, and a man of good taste, he admired the Scripture for its fine style no less than for its basic truth. The Port-Royal editors record in their *Préface*[50] that Pascal found 'elements of beauty, in the Gospels particularly, which it may be no one before him had ever noticed. The simplicity of Jesus' words impressed him above all else, and this he explained by saying that our Lord, finding His own spirit at home among the most sublime concerns of the Kingdom of God, was enabled to speak of the supernatural with the greatest naturalness. This lent a certain naïve candour to His words, a quality which is only added evidence of His divinity and in no sense contrary to it.

In Fragment 797 of the *Pensées* under the caption " Proofs of Jesus Christ," we read this charming tribute : " Jesus Christ said great things so simply, that it seems as though He had not thought them great; and yet so clearly that we can easily see what He thought of them. This clearness, joined to simplicity, is wonderful."[51] The succeeding fragment stresses the admirable style of the Gospels, and its unaffected modesty. " Who taught the Evangelists these same qualities of Christ," he asks in Fragment 800, " so that they could know how to portray with such nuance the very soul of Him? " Pascal immediately rejects the notion that the apostles could have been impostors,[52] deceived or deceivers.[53] His conclusion is that the glorified Christ continued to inspire His followers.[54] Pascal's eulogy of the style of the Bible takes the form of a characteristic lapidary formula : " God rightly speaks of God."[55]

Pascal's Bibles

Pascal most naturally uses the Vulgate Edition as his chief reference in studying Scripture, since it was, by virtue of a decree of the Council of Trent of April 8, 1546, the only authorized edition in the Roman Catholic Church. Thanks to the aid of Popes Sixtus V and Clement VIII, a revised and corrected text of the Vulgate had now been published, which was regarded as definite, and came to be known as the Sixto-Clementine Bible. This is the text to which Pascal, as a loyal Catholic, referred when he wrote the *Provinciales*, as well as

the *Ecrits des Curés de Paris* and the *Projet de Mandement*—
all drafted for the use of the French clergy. Being the only
authorized edition in the Church, it was the only one which
might be cited as proof. It will be recalled that the Vulgate
originated as the Latin version of the Bible, translated from
the Septuagint and corrected by Saint Jerome.

Pascal himself makes no reference to the Septuagint. He
set out directly from the Vulgate. He had a thorough knowledge of Latin and translated it freely, as is shown by the corrections and marginal notes in his manuscripts. Even in the
words he crossed out, we never find a mistranslation, but only
the minor corrections made by a busy man who was summarizing in French the details he found in the Latin text.

We should never lose sight of Pascal's realism. Always he
remained the practical man of Auvergne. Born in a town
where the neighbours made vegetables grow on an abandoned
moat, Pascal wanted things ever to be tangible and sure. He
put his questions to the Bible in just the way he had put them
to Nature, always keeping in mind the distinction between
what depended upon authority and what upon experimental
science.

Pascal often appeared to be a hasty worker, but this did not
mean that he neglected detail. Quite the contrary. The
matter in hand was far too important in his eyes for that. Just
as in the field of physics he had once exhausted every resource
of methodology, of proof, of counterproof, and of verification,
so now, as a student of the Bible, he neglected no source of
information or verification. As to the content of his inquiry,
he displayed great independence of mind, and seems to have
felt justified in turning to Protestant sources, and also to the
Jewish rabbis.

Whenever he was trying to restore the original form of a
Scriptural text so as to meet an objection, or to refute some
error, or to discomfit an unbelieving opponent, he was, we
find, dominated by a desire for purity of doctrine. In the Vulgate, for example, these are the words in which the irritated
Jews accused Jesus of blasphemy : *Quia tu, homo cum sis, facis
teipsum Deum*, taken from the Greek : ὅτι καὶ σὺ, ἄνθρωπος
ὢν, σαυτὸν ποιεῖς θεόν.* The Vulgate puts a conjunctional sub-
ordinate in place of the participial clause in the Greek, thus in-
troducing a slight sense of concession into the translation. It

* " Because that thou, being a man, makest thyself God " (John x. 33).

stresses the grounds for the grievance, rather than the incompatibility between the divine nature and the human nature. Pascal openly challenges the Latin genius, and observes an absolute literalism in his own translation : *Homo existens, Deum te facis.* He then devotes all his energy to meeting this objection, in order to show that Jesus' claim, as understood by the Jews, merely affirmed the identity underlying these contradictions, and thus led to an absurdity. Pascal's original translation was intended to shed some light upon the course of his reasoning,[56] and it succeeded in its aim.

Did Pascal consult the Hebrew Bible directly? It appears that, in addition to Saint Jerome's translation, he also used that of Vatable,[57] an " apostate " who had gone over to Protestantism. Pascal seems to have had some acquaintance with the Hebrew language. What he learned may have come from working with the *Polyglot Bible*, each page of which was printed in four parallel columns, including : (1) the Greek text of the Septuagint; (2) the Latin text of the Vulgate; (3) a new translation made from the Hebrew by Sante Pagnino; and (4) the Hebrew text itself. In the margin of the Greek text appeared a summary in Latin and a concordance of Biblical texts. At the bottom of each page were found, along with Vatable's notes, the diverse interpretations of the commentators, some passages translated by the Fathers, and occasionally a literal translation. " Thus arranged," so Lhermet points out, " Vatable's Bible had a double advantage : it was of great practical utility in that it assembled, one beside the other, all the texts recognized by the Church, at the same time taking account of other editions; secondly, it was scientifically useful, in that, by recording variant readings, it satisfied the inquiring and reasoning mind of Pascal, who made his own choice among them, selecting the one which conformed most closely to the ideas he was developing."[58] This is a fine tribute to this scholarly edition, edited by one of the royal lecturers appointed by Francis I, at the time when the latter was laying the foundation for what was to become the Collège de France. It will further be recalled that Calvin studied Hebrew under Vatable in 1531.

A Scrupulous Scholar

Lhermet was of the opinion, formed by selecting such texts as Fragment 434 of the *Pensées*, and more especially the quotation from Psalm cxviii. 13, that Pascal made use of a method of contamination in order to favour the Jansenist position. In Lhermet's view, Pascal was motivated less by the philologist's scruples in finding that translation which would keep most faithfully to the original, than by " the concern of a clever man who wanted to see the triumph of his religious ideas." Where necessary, Lhermet goes on to assert, Pascal resorted to omission and condensation, or borrowed from both versions, i.e., the Vulgate and the Vatable edition, according as the one or the other would bring to light some fact or establish some truth favouring the Jansenist position.[59]

In a very detailed study, published in the *Revue d'Histoire Littéraire de la France*,[60] Joseph Dedieu takes Lhermet to task on this point. In a devastating critique, he refutes point by point the charge that Pascal deliberately altered the sacred words of Scriptural tradition with a view to stressing or strengthening the Jansenist aspect of his *Vindication of Christianity*. Dedieu declares, first of all, that this accusation shocks every probability. It is no less a shock to " the whole uprightness, inflexible to the point of brutality, which this noble character displayed at every point in his work."[61] After examining closely the texts from the Vulgate, from Vatable, and from Pascal, Dedieu exposes the feebleness of the arguments put forward[62] and shows how very precise the translations of Pascal really were—even to the point of their Oriental manner of phrasing[63]—for Pascal was a scholar who had familiarized himself with the Hebrew commentaries.

Hence Pascal emerges greatly enhanced in stature from Dedieu's critique, which is fully documented. This Roman Catholic scholar of exegesis ends by denouncing the gravity of injustice and the fallacy in an entire school of thought, which is still, alas, deeply rooted in our time. This consists in regarding the theological Fragments of the *Pensées* with a measure of contempt. " Pascal brought all his powers of reflection and ingenuity to his study of the Scriptural text. He was familiar with every scholarly scruple and, I would add, retained his full freedom of mind as well. Had he had at his disposal the same knowledge of Hebrew matters that Spinoza had, it may well be that we should have had an extraordinary French version of the Bible."[64] Mauriac, another Roman Catholic writer, echoes Dedieu's view in doing belated justice to Pascal's good name, basing his own opinion upon the testimony of the admirable

Père Lagrange : " The contempt which has long been affected toward Pascal as an exegete cannot be sustained in view of the testimony of a scholar such as Père Lagrange : his arguments remain weighty down to our own day, even from the stand-point of modern exegesis."[65] Let us take the liberty of adding, since we have adduced authoritative testimony to counter-balance Lhermet's unfortunate statement, that Pascal himself once wrote a Fragment in the *Pensées* " against those who mis-use passages of Scripture and who pride themselves in finding one which seems to favour their error."[66] This should suffice to indicate the objectivity, the integrity, and the erudition of Pascal's research, which has at last received due homage.

The Bible of the " Mémorial "

Another type of question must now, however, be considered. The specific problem which confronts us here was raised by Strowski,[67] as we know, regarding the night of November 23, 1654. Pascal was fingering the pages of Scripture. The quota-tions in French, which form part of the *Mémorial*, stand in the archaic French of Lefèvre d'Etaples. Had Pascal been quoting from memory, he would have corrected the archaism of his phrases; but he did not do so.[68] Pascal was reading, then, from some French edition of the Bible. From which one?

In his brief study on *Pascal et la Bible*,[69] Jovy considers the leading French versions of the Bible which might have been used by families in Pascal's time. He lists thirteen titles. This list makes no reference, however, doubtless because of its Pro-testant origin, to the Bible prepared by the pastors and pro-fessors of the Church of Geneva, an edition of which we have a copy in our possession,[70] published at Saumur in 1614. A copy of this Geneva Bible might very well have found its way into the Pascal home, for we have already seen that some members of an earlier generation of the family were influenced, for a brief time, by Protestantism. Can we think of any Pro-testant family of such standing without its own Bible? Further-more, this Geneva Bible was the fruit of the best scholarly work of the Renaissance, and we have seen that Pascal's father was reared in Paris during the Renaissance. He was a man of ample good taste and would have doubtless treasured such a volume. He might very well have himself purchased a copy, if he should not have discovered one in his library. Blaise, indeed, was the sort of person who would have put it to good use; we have already noted his eclectic habits when it came to probing Scripture. A man who had not hesitated to look into Vatable would hardly have hesitated to read the Geneva Bible. It is a fact that the French text of John xii. 3, so often quoted in the words of the *Mémorial*, is found word for word in this Geneva edition. It may be that, so far as Pascal is concerned, the passage was drawn from some source common to all the French versions of that period.

These French versions can be traced back to the translation made early in the sixteenth century by Lefèvre d'Etaples. In successive revisions, it became the Louvain Bible first printed in Antwerp in 1534; in Louvain in 1550; by Christopher Plantin of Antwerp in 1578; by Buon of Paris in 1586; by Pillehotte of Lyon in 1603; by Ménard of Paris in 1639. Jovy traces evidence of still another version of the Louvain Bible in the Bible of René Benoist, curate of Saint-Eustache, later Bishop of Troyes.[71] To us it seems worth pointing out that the Bible named for the doctors of Louvain, published by Plantin in 1578 with a preface by Jacobin de Bay (1572), was very similar to the Bible of René Benoist,[72] and also to the Geneva version; and that all these versions were only variants of the evangelical one by Lefèvre d'Etaples, which accounts for their similarity. We may willingly admit that it was most probably a Catholic version that Blaise was reading on the night of November 23, 1654. Perhaps it was the Louvain edition or that of René Benoist. Since most of the Old Testament quotations in his writings are from the Louvain edition, we may presume that he read from it. This does not, however, exclude the probability that he had somewhere in his library a copy of the Geneva Bible which contains the exact form of John xii. 3 as Pascal quoted it in the *Mémorial*.

As Pascal studied the Scripture, he carefully consulted the commentaries of the rabbis,[73] and one of the concordances— *concordantiae utriusque testamentii*—which were already in wide circulation at the time. He made use of certain books of maxims, prayers, and Christian teachings, drawn from both Testaments, perhaps in manuscript form. One of his letters gives evidence of this.[74] We know also how frequently he read the same books as Jacqueline, and we know that in the course of her examination on August 22, 1661, she answered a questioner concerning the books she read: "At present it is the *Morales* of St. Basil who is seldom translated." She was referring to the *Règles de la Morale Chrestienne*, selected from the New Testament by Saint Basil, with accompanying explanations by Guillaume le Roy. Finally, we know that Pascal was fearful of the charge of heresy. This accounts for the meticulous verification of all his Biblical inquiries by reference to the Fathers and to tradition. This may be illustrated by Fragment 775 of the *Pensées*, which concludes in these words: " We must, then, follow the Fathers and tradition in order to know when [we must explain *omnes* by *all*] to do so, since there is heresy to be feared on both sides." (He was concerned with two verses of Scripture, Matthew xxvi. 27 and Romans v. 12.) Pascal clearly manifested great scruple and caution in studiously searching Holy Scripture.

Translating Scripture

It should be understood that Pascal never claimed to give a full translation from the Bible. That was not his primary aim. There were indeed lengthy translations from his own pen, as in Fragments 682, 713, 722, 726, of the *Pensées*; but, whether long or short, these translations had but a single purpose, to probe into this or that point of Scripture either for personal edification or to shed light upon some matter with which Pascal was concerned at the time. It was Pascal's aim which determined the particular method he chose to employ.

Thus we see that his chief concern was, at one and the same time, to prove loyal to the message once delivered to the saints and intelligible to his own contemporaries by speaking in a language they could understand. Knowing the inadequacy of the translations at his disposal, he turned so far as possible to the originals, seeking to draw their message directly and in as literal a form as he could. At the same time, being an *honnête homme* in a cultured society, he omitted certain details which might have shocked his readers, and in certain instances adapted his phrases to the tastes of his time. In Amos viii. 10, for example, he omitted the reference to the figure of a father mourning for his only son, with sackcloth on his back and his head shaven. In Isaiah l. 23 he changed the words, " *Lick* up the dust of thy feet," to, " *Kiss* the dust of thy feet." He did not elaborate the detailed account of the idols, and passed over in silence the false gods and pagan sacrifices, when it did no injury to the sense of the passage.[75]

Whenever some point of doctrine was involved, however,

Pascal was rigorously faithful to the text. Thus it was that he retained the entire description of the image in Daniel,[76] for this concerned an important point of prophecy. In his arguments one feels that he was drawing upon the legal tradition of his family, cutting out useless details, selecting and arranging the Scripture passages he needed in preparing for a verbal assault upon some position held by his opponent. Occasionally he introduced a relative pronoun or conjunction into the Scripture text, aiming to clarify some clause which required some special emphasis. Isaiah xli. 23 came to read, at his hands, " If *ye are gods*, draw near, show us the things that are to come hereafter . . . ; *by this token we shall know* ye are gods."[77] Spurred on by the intuitive mind (*esprit de finesse*), the mathematical genius went so far as to introduce into Scripture a logical structure which was not originally there, or which at most was perhaps implied. In giving voice to this logic of the inner man, Pascal was once again a child of his age.

He would add emphasis to some word in the text, in a wholly Biblical spirit, in order to lend new force to its message. The " *Dabo vobis cor novum* " (" A new heart will I give you ") of the Vulgate thus became " *Je créerai en vous un cœur nouveau* " (" A new heart will I create within you "). Pascal shortens, omits, adds, annotates, comments, combines texts, and inserts his own interpretation. Obscure passages of prophecy are clarified by the light of history for this man to whom a measure of understanding has been granted by " the hidden God." Pascal's translation thus amounted to a paraphrase of Scripture. But, make no mistake, this habit of paraphrase was always for a reason, namely, to lead men to accept Scripture as nearly as possible in its literal form. This was in fact the method in use at Port-Royal, and M. de Saci regularly employed it.

Let us see exactly how Pascal worked upon a passage such as Fragment 722 of the *Pensées*, which we mentioned above briefly. It has reference to Daniel xi. 2 : " The angel said to Daniel : There shall stand up (after Cyrus, under whom this still is) three Kings in Persia (Cambyses, Smerdis, Darius), and the fourth, who shall then come (Xerxes), shall be far richer than they all, and far stronger, and shall stir up all his people against the Greeks."[78] Now compare this with the Biblical text : " Behold there shall stand up three kings in Persia, and the fourth shall be enriched exceedingly above them all : and

when he shall be grown mighty by his riches, he shall stir up
all against the kingdom of Greece." Pascal's version is briefer.
He introduces it by the words: " The angel said to Daniel,"
and the direct nature of the divine message is made quite clear.
The interpretation he adds for the sake of clarification : " There
shall stand . . . three kings of Persia," and " the fourth."
And Pascal goes on, by way of strengthening this point, to
add, " Who shall then come," reaching the climax of this prophecy in disclosing the full prospect: " And shall stir up his
people against the Greeks." Pascal was concerned for the
quasi-mathematical exactness of prophecy, as it came to be
verified point by point. To this extent translation became for
him a form of Bible study, properly speaking, and the translation itself became a secondary concern. Let us now turn to
this aspect of Pascal's work.

Probing Scripture

As a student of the Bible, Pascal had his favourite verses,
to which he continually turned. One of these was the famous
text of Daniel ix. 24. At the end of Fragment 692 of the
Pensées, he summarized it in a concise, abbreviated form,
which brings out the essential point. The reference to *ever-
lasting justice*, however, strikes Pascal's religious consciousness, and he proceeds to insert a brief comment of his own :
" *Eternal* justice, not legal, but eternal."[79] We know how
often Pascal was to recur to this theme of true Justice, within
the order of charity, which he held to be opposed to the notion
of arbitrary, capricious, human forms of justice, within the
order of the mind. This higher notion we find that he took
from the Bible, or perhaps he nourished from Biblical sources
a notion already dear to him. In the study of his Bible, as we
have said, he now gave the same attention to minute detail that
he once applied in his study of Nature. In Fragment 636 of
the *Pensées* we see with what care he examined Malachi ii. 2
and Isaiah i. 19, probably in the light of Genesis ii. 17. " *If* does
not indicate indifference : Malachi, Isaiah, Is., *Si volumus,* etc.
In quacumque die."[80]

How was a man to understand Scripture? It required,
indeed, the grace of God. But where did man's part begin?
Put the question to Scripture itself : The mysteries have there
been revealed to us in a certain order. In the same way, this
order must be followed in the case of every individual. The

Jews learned the meaning of repentance before they learned of grace. John the Baptist came before Jesus Christ. In the same way, it is by repentance, again, that the individual Christian attains to faith, to charity, to grace.[81] The converse is also true, namely, that no one abandons the truth as it is in Scripture "save by abandoning charity."

What is needed, therefore, in *conversion* in the literal sense of the word? We "had our own will as our rule. Let us now take the will of [God]."[82] Repentance is thus the key to true understanding, and all valid psychology, having to do with human understanding as well as with other activity, derives its basic principle from the Gospel. "The veil, which is upon these books for the Jews, is there also for evil Christians, and for all who do not hate themselves."[83] Only a faith born of repentance is sufficient to break the vicious circle willed by a hidden God: Prophecies "are proofs only to those who know and believe them."[84] The paradox is a divine paradox. Blessed are those who have eyes to see!

In his study of the Bible, Pascal followed a method which is familiar enough to men of God: It consisted in grouping a series of texts around a single question. Thus the author of the *Imitation of Christ* (III, lviii. 9) brings together two texts from Isaiah (ch. lx. 22 and ch. lxv. 20), when he states the principle: "The least shall become a thousand, and the sinner of an hundred years shall die," aiming to point out that we must not seek to penetrate truth which is above us, nor the secret judgments of God. We find Pascal, similarly, examining such a question as sanctification in Section XIV of the *Pensées*. We find here thirty-five selected texts crowded into a single Fragment.[85] Again we find him listing, within a single Fragment, seven texts in less than ten lines, as he considers the Christian's triumph over death![86] We could go on citing examples of this kind to illuminate his method. The *Abrégé de la Vie de Jésus-Christ*, cited above in these pages, furnishes a choice example. Both in his quotations and in his translations, Pascal at one time is quite precise and complete while at another time he abbreviates; now he adds a phrase of comment, now he changes the order of words; now he groups together selections from varied passages by the same author; now he quotes Old Testament passages following those from the New, now he weaves together sections drawn from both; and then again he borrows from the commentaries in Vatable's

Polyglot Bible. When he feels he must bring to a climax some argument, in which his quotations have found their place within a structure of pitiless logic, Pascal may suddenly disregard altogether the text of the Book he has been examining so meticulously, and rely for the time being wholly upon his memory. Dedieu has listed no less than thirty-eight passages in the first twelve sections of the *Pensées*[87] that are faulty in this respect. In such cases, the passionate Pascal is simply carried away by the end he has in view.

The Last Prophet of Israel

All the while, however, there is no break in continuity, no interruption in the smoothly flowing style, so rich in the life-blood it has drawn from the Bible itself. Pascal's style is now that of the prophet, now that of a poet, now that of an orator, then that of a man of law—or, we may say, a man of God's law. After a section marked by gradual growth, there is suddenly an upsurge of energy overflowing in all its abundance. Such, for example, are the ejaculatory prayers like the *Mystère de Jésus*, in which, as Charles Du Bos finely describes it, " the sombre rhythm of contrition is akin to a certain adagio in one of the later Beethoven quartets."[88] Ernest Havet felt with regard to Pascal's translation of Isaiah, ch. xlix, that he could speak of it as a masterpiece, gathering up all the inspiration found in this, perhaps the most magnificent text in the whole of the sacred writings.[89] With unfailing good taste, Pascal borrows from the Bible such words as may lend vivid colour to his own discourse. Instead of the Greek χάος, he prefers ἀχάσμα which he translates *gouffre immense* (immense chasm). He selects from the Bible innumerable figures of speech, drawn in the language of flesh and blood, filled with vital energy. He enriches his diction with Hebrew phrases, and his style with a poesy flowing with robust strength and ample sympathy. The Biblical elements are so intricately interwoven with the threads of his own thought that they lend an incomparable richness to the texture of his phrasing. He writes :

" Les Juifs avaient vieilli dans ces pensers terrestres, que Dieu aimait leur père Abraham, sa chair qui en sortait; que pour cela il les avait multipliés et distingués de tous les autres peuples, sans souffrir qu'ils s'y mêlassent; que, quand ils languissaient en Egypte, il les en rétira avec tous ses grands signes en leur faveur; qu'il les nourrit de la manne dans le désert; qu'il les mena dans une terre bien grasse; qu'il leur donna des rois et un temple bien bâti pour y offrir des bêtes, et par le moyen de leur sang qu'ils seraient purifiés, et qu'il leur devait envoyer le Messie pour les rendre maîtres de tout le monde, et il a prédit le temps de sa venue.

"Le monde ayant vieilli dans ses erreurs charnelles, Jésus-Christ est venu dans le temps prédit, mais non pas dans l'éclat attendu; et ainsi ils n'ont pas pensé que ce fût lui."[90]

Translated: "The Jews had grown old in these earthly thoughts; that God loved their father Abraham, and the seed that came after him; that on account of this He had made them to multiply and had set them apart from all other peoples, and yet would not allow them to intermingle; that when they were languishing in Egypt, He brought them out with all His great signs in their favour; that He fed them with manna in the wilderness; that He led them to a rich and fertile land; that He gave to them kings and a temple solidly built for them to make offerings of beasts, by the shedding of whose blood they should be purified; and that He would send them a Messiah to make them masters of all the world; and foretold the time of His coming.

"The world having grown old in these carnal errors, Jesus Christ came at the time foretold, but not in the expected magnificence; and thus they did not think that it was He."

Pascal was the very first author, before Bossuet, Racine, La Fontaine, Rousseau, or Chateaubriand, to introduce music, painting, and imitative harmony into French prose, together with all the wealth of imagery drawn from a life at once human and divine. "With him art passes into genius, to such a point that to call him an artist would be to do him an injury."[91]

In a splendid chapter on "Pascal as Poet," Dr. H. F. Stewart has furnished us with a first-class analysis to which the reader is referred. In a time when strong emotion was absent from verse, Blaise Pascal the prose writer was, according to Stewart, "an authentic poet, and most poetical when he drew his inspiration from the book which above all else he valued and studied, the Bible."[92] Stewart insists, for example, on Pascal's use of prosopopoeia, a method of personification dear to the Hebrews. A further feature of Hebrew poetry, he adds, is "the parallelism which gives it its peculiar force and rhythmical music. This was congenial to Pascal's genius, and the practice

of it colours many pages of his prose."[93]   The Bible provided
Pascal also with a peculiar notion of *le cœur* (the heart), as
being " the sense of the inner depth of human nature, of the
seat of knowledge and will."   This notion was indeed enriched by Pascal's own experience, and became strikingly
similar to our notion of intuition.   Its original meaning, however, roots deep in the Book.   In his conclusion, Stewart praises
Pascal's masterpieces " as literature immortal, and as language,
setting the example whereby French prose has become the most
perfect vehicle of lucid and persuasive speech which men have
used since the days of Plato and Demosthenes."   Pascal is
" a living force."   To read him is " an inspiration precisely
because he speaks with the voice of the inspired prophet and
poet, seeing the truth with the single eye which receives and
radiates the light."

   The light which radiated from Pascal was, in fact, a light
which he had received with singleness of heart through the
pages of the Holy Book : " There is enough light for those
whose only desire is to see," he used to say modestly, once
he had found his way to the Pool of Siloam.

IV
RUNNING THE WAY OF THE LORD

*I will run the way of thy commandments, when thou shalt
enlarge my heart.* PSALM CXIX. 32

In a broad sense Blaise Pascal was committed as a writer to the
cause of Christianity, and in this respect he belongs to his century. The great classic writers of the period, who seem at first
glance to have been utterly removed from religious preoccupa-
tion, among them Descartes, Corneille, Racine, Boileau, La
Fontaine, Mme de La Fayette, La Bruyère, and La Rochefoucauld, are in reality just as Christian as they are French. In
their work there rise to the surface, more unconsciously than
otherwise, certain " anxieties, scruples, revolts, and fine points
of heroism or of perversity, that were either unknown to the
ancients or completely scorned by them. . . . Chateaubriand's
insight did not fail him when he recognized in the Andro-
mache or in the Iphigenia of Racine the Christian wife and
daughter."[1] More than once have Pascal's sisters, Gilberte
and Jacqueline, reminded us of some of Racine's heroines. So
Pascal himself exemplified the eagerness and profundity of the
Christian man of letters.

A Christian Layman

This he showed more directly when he wrote the *Provinciales*
and when he collaborated in the translation of the Mons edition
of the New Testament, cited in our previous chapter, and
which, we remember, was chiefly the work of his spiritual
adviser, Monsieur de Saci.[2] In Pascal, it was " the whole
man " that brought to fruition the great, divinely appointed
task of planting the love of Christ in the hearts of men, a task
which was to become his lifework. One of the first Christian
laymen, Pascal revealed himself as that passionate lover of
truth,[3] " that poet who preaches salvation with such despair,
. . . that angel of light . . . , that inspired rebel," whom the
modern Church distrusts.[4] He is the man of the Bible clutch-
ing by the lapel of his coat the free-thinker whom he would
shake into consciousness, the lost sheep who turns his eyes away

from the only thing which counts in this world : the problem of human destiny and that other so completely inseparable from it, the problem of individual salvation.   Pascal is the family man, the friend, true enough, the guardian of the weak in faith, the letter writer who offers spiritual advice.   But above all, he is a committed Christian scholar who would devote the strength that is left him to writing on a new basis, entirely Biblical in inspiration, a vindication of religion.   He is the elect of God, highly conscious of his responsibility.

He knows it : " From the one who has received the most, shall the greatest account be demanded, because of the power which he has through the help [of Grace]."[5] He read that and meditated on it in Luke xii. 47 and in Revelations xxii. 11. Henceforth, his greatest desire, according to a beautiful expression that we find in a fragment of his *Pensées*, is " to beget children for God."[6] He knows that the meaning of the Greek word ἁμαρτάνειν, to sin, is to err, to miss the mark, and he pities " those miserable lost ones, who having looked around and having seen some pleasant objects, have surrendered to such things, and have become attached to them."[7]

Certainly, he also knows quite well that it is grace which must bring about the transformation of the unbeliever, and engender faith in him.[8] He read in chapter x of The Epistle of Paul to the Romans, verse 17, " Faith then cometh by hearing; and hearing by the word of Christ." Preaching appears to him essentially a message of salvation which must be announced. It is in this sense that we are labourers together with God. This state of things leaves, and Pascal admits it, an infinite part to mystery which we cannot claim to encompass. We already know to what point Pascal respects the apparent antinomies of the Scriptures : salvation comes from God . . . work out your salvation; yet he holds solidly to both ends of the chain, whose central links are not all visible to him. It is to misunderstand Pascal greatly, to suggest, by drawing arguments from his project of a *Vindication of Christianity*, that in his heart he did not believe in election, and that on this point in particular he " did not belong to Port-Royal." Pascal believed in election for this very reason, i.e., that election is formally taught in the Bible, whether that pleases us or not, we who like to set ourselves up as little gods. The great battle of Christianity through all the ages is " being fought by two invisible armies, as they struggle to dominate the minds of men.

The one army we might rightly call Supernaturalism; the other, with equal accuracy, we shall designate Naturalism."[9] In this battle, Pascal is clearly on the side of supernaturalism in all that touches questions of faith. That is why we have seen him oppose to scholasticism a theology strictly Biblical.

Unbelievers, exactly on this point, take argument from the objections which reason is bold enough to oppose to the Christian interpretation of the Bible. The fact is, however, that nothing should frighten them " like that revolt of reason against the authority of the word of God revealed: is it not the sign that one is excluded and reproved? "[10]

According to Mme Périer, his sister, when Pascal conferred with unbelievers, he began by seeking to discover " if they were looking for truth with all their hearts."[11] Then he measured, disposed, and expressed what he had to say to them, to make it enter their spirit.[12] At the school of his Master, and in his name, he stood at the door and knocked. The door partly opened, he entered with an argumentation in which were found disposed for the greater glory of God all his acquisitions: " a whole unity of views on nature, science and man," which *alone*, as he saw it, were in accord with " faith, once accepted," and which *alone* could " lead the indifferent or the unbeliever to faith."[13] It was thus that he was able to despoil theology " of a whole repulsive exterior apparatus and present it in an engaging manner, and to speak the language of the seventeenth century, in a *polite* way."[14]

For this God-appointed task, Pascal prepared himself with the greatest care. His *Pensées* on rhetoric testify to this. In his fragment *De l'Art de Persuader*, he had, moreover, taken care, from the beginning, to set aside the divine truths as being so far above Nature that only God Himself could introduce them into the soul in any way which might please Him. " I know," wrote Pascal then—probably toward 1658-1659—that " in order to humiliate that superb power of reasoning which claims it must be judge of the things which the will chooses, and to cure that infirm will, [God wished] that these truths enter from the heart to the mind, and not from the mind to the heart." That is the reason one says of human things that one must know them before one can love them, while according to the saints one must love divine things in order to know them, for one enters into truth only through charity.

This psychological approach should be understood in the

framework of the Pascalian orders to which we have paid so
much attention in these pages. It appears to Pascal that " God
established that supernatural order, quite contrary to the order
which should be natural to men in the things of nature. They
have nevertheless corrupted that order by making of profane
things what they should have made of sacred things because
we believe almost nothing except what pleases us. And from
there comes the fact that we are so far from consenting to the
truths of the Christian religion, absolutely opposed as they are
to our pleasures. *Tell us agreeable things and we shall listen
to you,* said the Jews to Moses, as if agreeableness should regu-
late belief! "[15] It is by such pages that Pascal, after the author
of the *Imitation of Christ,* has convinced us that all true
psychology has its principle in the Bible.

Pascal's apologetics are Scriptural, in the spirit and in the
letter. In his *Comparaison des Chrétiens des Premiers Temps
avec ceux d'Aujourd'hui,* Pascal asks that catechumens submit
themselves not only to instruction, but also to penitence.[16]
From their very first steps, Pascal would have those whom he
touches know that they ought not to say, " I would soon leave
my way of life if I had faith," but rather, " I should soon have
faith if I were to leave my way of life." Pascal is closely
attached to the family of Arnobe, of Lactantius, and of Saint
Augustine. It is their true method which he found again
through a happy intuition, the method which is originally in
the New Testament and in Saint Paul, the one which the first
apostles and the first Church Fathers practised, and which
made the strength and the success of the apologists of the third
and fourth centuries. " In the history of modern apologetics,
Pascal is as great a name as Socrates in the history of ancient
philosophy."[17]

For Pascal, it is not a question of more or less in " conversion " taken in its exact meaning : it is a miracle where
" efficacious grace " intervenes, the very grace which brought
Jesus back to life. And it is indeed a question of a passage
from death to life for the regenerated man. The opuscule *Sur
la Conversion du Pécheur* presents reminiscences of the Sermon
on the Mount.[18] Pascal's opposition of the heart to the mind
is a résumé of " the opposition between the action which God
exercises on man and the action of which man reduced to his
own strength is capable."[19] Thus, this opposition has a claim
to the very heart of Pascal's apologetics.

For this Christian layman, every choice which daily life brings up is resolved by an appeal to the Bible. When it is a question of a proposed marriage for his niece, Jacqueline Périer, Pascal writes to her a letter filled with the doctrine of Saint Paul.[20] To Domat, who needs encouragement for the common struggle in the service of Jansenist truth, he addressed a message in which Saint John and Saint Paul are cited as testimony.[21]

What inspires him is Christian charity, victorious, if need be, over prejudice. We see him rendering the most gracious homage to a Protestant—in the person of the doctor attached to Mme du Sablé, who has remained famous for her dread of contagion. Menjot, the Protestant doctor, embarrassed by such homage coming from Blaise Pascal, wrote on this subject to Mme du Sablé: " If, on one hand, I consider the sincerity and the sublime knowledge of that great man, on the other hand I know that charity is the first of Christian virtues, so that I have difficulty in distinguishing between justice and grace principally in a person who doubtless puts it into practice with as much ardour as he sustains it."[22] Menjot was not mistaken: This took place in 1660, and Pascal had long since renounced the advantages which politeness alone can give in worldly relations: it was indeed Christian charity which inspired him above all.

A thing which inspired him still more, and which inspired his charity and all the aims and views which this charity crowned, was his idea of God the Sovereign Good and Master of all things. A contemporary Protestant writer, Loraine Boettner, justly wonders at a letter of Pascal " to a bereaved friend." Instead of repeating the ordinary platitudes of consolation, Pascal develops here the beautiful Biblical theme of the decrees of Providence, in these terms: " If we regard this event, not as an effect of chance, not as a fatal necessity of nature, but as a result inevitable, just, holy, of a decree of His Providence, conceived from all eternity, to be executed in such a year, day, hour and such a place and manner, we shall adore in humble silence the impenetrable loftiness of His Secrets: we shall venerate the sanctity of His decrees: we shall bless the acts of His Providence; and uniting our will to that of God Himself, we shall wish with Him, the thing that He has willed in us and for us for all eternity."[23] Loraine Boettner is mistaken, however: The letter in question is the letter which

Pascal wrote to his elder sister, Mme Périer, and to her husband, on the death of Etienne Pascal, their father, October 17, 1651. The translation which Boettner gives of it is garbled and incomplete, as one can realize by referring to the original.[24] Yet these considerations take nothing from the value of the argument, and in certain respects accentuate its force. Sabatier, studying predestination in the Apostle Paul, noted in particularly fortunate terms, that it is "a normal product of religious faith," and that the feeling of predestination "never grows weaker without bringing or marking an equal weakening" of this very faith.[25] This assertion finds its full weight under the pen of a liberal Protestant. One must add, for the case of Pascal, the fact that theological determinism presents a particular attraction for a man of science.

In the political realm also, our Christian layman is dominated by this same viewpoint of the decrees of Providence. We find him, toward 1659, haunted by the idea of a theocracy of Biblical inspiration, apropos of *Trois Discours sur la Condition des Grands*. Nicole had had the three opuscules of Pascal preceded by this notice: "One of the things on which the late M. Pascal had many views was the instruction of a Prince, whom one should try to raise in the manner most fitting to the state where God calls him, and the most proper to make him capable of fulfilling all the duties and avoid all of the dangers of this state. He has often been heard to say that there was nothing to which he desired to contribute more if he were to become engaged in it, and that he would willingly sacrifice his life for such an important thing."[26] In the meantime, he consecrated this life to bringing forth children for God and to making himself their spiritual guardian.

Spiritual Guidance

The best example of Pascal in this role is doubtless furnished us by the instance of the Duke and Mlle de Roannez. Pascal led to God the Duke who, in his pursuit of saintliness, subsequently was to resign from his governorship of Poitou, and to give up his plan of marrying Mlle de Mesme, a rich heiress. For those who know the views on the "bondage of marriage" to which Pascal had come,[27] the latter's influence on his friend the Duke is in this circumstance evident. The Count d'Harcourt, great-uncle of the Duke, knew this quite well. Doubtless it was he who had encouraged the wife of the concierge of the Roannez household to attack Pascal with a knife while he was in bed. The attempt was fruitless, however, for that morning Pascal had already left his bed to go to church! Mlle de Roannez herself was to refuse the hand of the Marquis d'Alluyre. Already under the influence of her brother, and more or less directly under that of Blaise who perhaps in the course of his " worldly " period had cast his eyes on her, she nurtured vague desires to become a nun. It was during the mass celebrating the miracle of the Holy Thorn, in the course of which she had not ceased to shed tears, that Mlle de Roannez had felt her vocation take form. And it was upon coming home that she had announced her decision to give up marriage and enter a convent. Her family were not able to make her change her mind. Pascal became henceforth the spiritual adviser of the brother and the sister : " I do not separate you two, and I think constantly of both of you," he wrote to them Sunday, November 5, 1656.[28]

These letters of guidance are a beautiful Christian inspiration. Upon reading them objectively, one can indeed find passages which could be interpreted in the light of an attachment not entirely forgotten of Blaise for Mlle de Roannez.[29] But from there to the interpretations which Chamaillard solicits from the texts,[30] there is a far cry. What do we know specifically on the subject of Pascal in love? Let us answer in all frankness : absolutely nothing. And let us add, moreover, that if Pascal thought of marriage on several occasions, that fact would offer nothing whatsoever which could contradict the interpretation that we offer here of his life. On the contrary, it has always pleased us to recognize that Pascal knew all our human vicissitudes. On the subject of Mlle de Roannez and her brother, if we respect the available texts, we can only affirm with Mauriac that Blaise Pascal belonged to his century, which was par excellence one of friendship.[31] The love of which he speaks, when he speaks of it abstractly is, moreover, that noble Cornelian love which is based on esteem.[32]

The themes of Pascal's letters of guidance to M. and Mlle de Roannez are rich in Christian counsel, for example, that the will of God must be our rule of life;[33] that renewal of heart gives fresh meaning to speech[34]—a Biblical expression taken from Ezekiel xviii. 31; xxxvi. 26, and from Mark xvi. 17; also the theme of the death of the old man and the renewal of the new man who will be perfect only in eternity, when he will sing the new song of which David speaks in Psalm cxlix. 1, the song of charity.[35]

Charlotte de Roannez was to enter Port-Royal in 1657, and remain there in spite of the violent objections of her family. Deprived of spiritual support by the death of Pascal in 1662 and of M. Singlin in 1664, and because of other circumstances which we shall not discuss here, Mlle de Roannez had herself relieved of her vows by Rome in 1665. Then, through the intercession of the king, she married the Duke de la Feuillade. The marriage had scarcely been consummated when she was to weep bitterly for her mistake before God. Her first child died at birth; her second was an invalid; her third, a dwarf, died at nineteen years; the race was miserably extinguished with the fourth. The poor mother had to undergo horrible operations, and these sad events make one diagnose a venereal disease in the Duke de la Feuillade, whose " gay " past was notorious. The Duchess died in 1683. At the hour of her death, her letters from Port-Royal were burned[36] and this destruction, as one may well think, has been shamefully exploited by those who are pleased to tell a romantic story of Mlle de Roannez and Pascal. Supposing that there were in the drawer of the cabinet of the Duchess de la Feuillade " compromising " secrets, is it good taste to speculate thus on the letters which an unhappy and repentant woman had burned on her deathbed? The seventeenth century certainly would not have pronounced *honnête* this way of doing things. It is true that we have evolved since then.

Vindication of Christianity

Further to spread the influence of his spiritual guidance,[37] Pascal was thinking more and more of writing a great work for the vindication of the Christian religion. His design took form in his mind toward 1658, when he consented to sketch in about two hours the outlines of his projected work for some of his Port-Royal friends. About eight years after Pascal's oral exposé, with the aid of the late scholar's notes, Filleau de la Chaise was to undertake to edit the *Discours sur les Pensées* in which Pascal's design appeared.[38] To carry out this plan Pascal, by his own confession, would have needed ten years of good health. However, since the spring of 1658, his health, which had never been good, became very poor. It was in order to distract his mind from horrible headaches that he turned again to mathematics and solved the insoluble problem of the cycloid.[39] The controversy which ensued lasted until the beginning of 1659 and tired Pascal a great deal. Before his death he had had at the most scarcely a year, and that in delicate health, to work on this vindication of Christianity which he loved more than any of the other works which he had done up to that time.

Of his efforts, what remains for us? Piles of papers on which he had feverishly jotted down or dictated notes, maxims, analyses that were pasted on registers, and which Etienne Pascal, nephew of Blaise, later had copied by secretaries. Port-Royal gave the first edition (posthumous) in 1670, which in its omissions and arrangements already constituted a Jansenist commentary on Pascal. In his superb edition, Brunschvicg presents to us the results of the examination of the manuscript copies; he tells us in detail about the preparation of the first edition; he gives us information on the composition of the examining committee and follows the fortunes of the later editions.[40] Each of these in some particular is found to be just another of the many commentaries on the thought of Pascal.

Modestly, Brunschvicg contents himself with classifying the fragments according to the main subjects which they treat. Doing this, he is obliged to separate thoughts which resemble each other in more than one aspect, even if they differ in others; on the other hand, he brings together other thoughts in ways that might distort the intention of the author.

The thought of Pascal thus broken up cannot but seem vague and incoherent! "Pascal incoherent!" cries Dr. Stewart indignantly: "he who was of an implacable coherence!" And the Cambridge professor submits a new suggestion which would consist in keeping of the *Pensées* only the fragments destined by Pascal to his *Vindication*, by classifying them according to the plan of Filleau de la Chaise.[41] Brunschvicg, however, had already replied to that suggestion, that the *Discours sur les Pensées* "does not have sufficient authority" to permit the restoration in question, and he has basis for this objection.[42]

Professor Stewart, however, pursues his efforts in the direction he has indicated. Already, in his fine collection of sermons entitled *Holiness of Pascal*,[43] he had felt that the page on the three orders leads us to the very centre of Pascal's thought. For

Pascal religious certainty was of the order of charity, super-natural. Reason of itself could not attain unto it. All that it could do was to prepare the way, first by analysing its own limitations, then by grouping auxiliary evidence, always in-sufficient in itself, that would confirm the intuition of the heart —this last word being understood in the Pascalian sense. This intuition, in turn, presupposes a man who proceeds in his search through labouring anguish. What Pascal wanted to do above all was to bring about both this labour and this anguish.

It is in following these broad outlines that Stewart, after so many others—among whom should be mentioned Strowski, Chevalier, Massis, Dedieu, Tourneur[44]—has just undertaken to finish the unfinished symphony, i.e., the *Vindication of Christianity*. In 1942, he published at the Cambridge Univer-sity Press the work which was to crown his noble efforts, under the title *Pascal's Apology for Religion Extracted from the* Pensées.[45]

It leaves one in deep thought to see what has here been selected as the " first *Pensée* " of Pascal, the fragment which, in the classification of Brunschvicg, is found under number 185. We must confess that it constitutes an excellent intro-duction : " The way of God, Who does all things in gentle-ness, is to instil religion into the mind through reasons, and into the heart through grace."[46]

We indeed grant this Cambridge professor that too many writers have strained the meaning by incorporating into the *Vindication* certain fragments which did not belong there. Certain fragments expressed the objections of free-thinkers that Pascal reproduced or imagined; others constituted arguments attributed by Pascal to some imaginary conferee, but with which he was far from being in agreement. What final criterion do we have at hand which will permit us to exercise the necessary discrimination? And then, how many hetero-geneous elements there are in the *Pensées*! We find there, for example, notes taken with the *Provinciales* in view, rough sketches of the same *Provinciales*, or of *Factums*.[47] Let us go farther. Here is something that appears essential to us : according to the most trustworthy testimony of Mar-guerite Périer, Pascal never forgot any of the ideas that crossed his mind, and he carried them in his memory up to the moment when he would make use of them. It was only in the last five years of his life—we would remind the reader of his fatigue and his deplorable state of health after 1658—that, "in order to relieve his mind," he cast on paper the thoughts which came to him. Fragment 370 of the *Pensées* offers here a curious testimony: "Chance gives thoughts, and chance takes them away: no art to conserve them nor to acquire them.

"Thought escapes, I wished to write it; I write instead that it has escaped me."[48]

What we suspect Pascal to have noted in the course, let us say, of the last five years of his life, would not therefore necessarily be thoughts bearing the date of these five years, but resurgences, reminiscences of thoughts acquired during the course of a laborious evolution belonging to almost his entire life. But let us take the question from another angle: Marguerite Périer—all of these Pascals are passionate people prone to exaggeration—stresses too strongly the fact that her uncle relied in normal times on his memory. We have had occasion to notice Pascal's habit of jotting rapid notes on tablets. He did this, for example, in the company of Méré, Miton, and Roannez at the time of their famous voyage to Poitou. Many of these notes must have been saved with the others. Certainly, he must have drawn from them in writing his *Vindication*—he who used everything that came his way. But that is not the question as, from both sides, we arrive at the conclusion that *the papers found after the death of Blaise Pascal, and today published under the title* Pensées, *constitute essentially the "journals" of a life as brief as it was fertile and full of genius.*

We have waited for this point in our development to justify our drawing so liberally from the *Pensées* in the course of our chapters. *In a way, a biographical study of Pascal would provide an excellent basis for a classification and an interpretation of the* Pensées *according to a psychological method.* All true psychology, for Pascal, has its starting-point in religion. Viewed in this light, the *Pensées* would then reveal their Biblical structure: *they constitute the mirror of a life lived and meditated more and more in the light of Scripture.*

Without doubt, since it is founded on facts, such an approach would explain, and consequently conciliate, numerous points of view. It is certain, for example, that there is a place, on the one hand, for an organic classification of all the *Pensées* considered as the whole of the journals of Blaise Pascal; on the other hand, for a selection of the type which Dr. Stewart is undertaking with a view to restoring the *Vindication of Chris-*

84 THE CLUE TO PASCAL

tianity. Not only are all these efforts praiseworthy in themselves, but they constitute just so many commentaries on Pascal.

An essential prerequisite of any restoration should be the relative importance that the Bible has in the fragments considered; the most profoundly Biblical will reveal a later composition. Who knows? Perhaps a pertinent organic classification of the *Pensées* should take as its starting-point (in memory of Pascal's childhood—which we have called his emergence) silhouettes of judges, of people in law courts, and the fragments treating a human conception of justice. Justice is a minimum of goodness and is only this world's conception of true charity. Our classification of the *Pensées* of this *honnête homme*, Blaise Pascal, would then be spread out between a human ideal, in large part inherited, and the soaring of the eagle's flight at the end. When Henri Bremond suggests that one take from " Pascal in prayer " fragments for a *Book of Hours*, he retains nothing for the Catholic heritage except the last outpourings of a consecrated soul longing for communion with the Christ. It is a delicate task indeed to draw dividing lines in the midst of such abounding wealth. Let us therefore keep an open mind as we consider existing outlines of the *Pensées*, and we may thereby expect a truer perspective of the aims of Pascal.

Biblical Structure of the *Pensées*

First of all, as we have said, the manuscript of the *Pensées* is a formless mass of papers. In a good article in *Comoedia*,[49] Strowski brings out the fact that these papers had been confided to a bookbinder—and at that time bookbinders did not know how to read. This bookbinder then cut and pared them down to make them occupy the least possible space. Next he pasted them hit-or-miss, like puzzles, on a big album of about five hundred pages. How idle, then, and misleading, is it to speculate on the varying margins of the manuscript!

The intimate history of the vicissitudes of a manuscript thus disposed is told us in detail by Guy de Pourtalès, in a carefully documented study,[50] which renders fine homage to the edition of Port-Royal. Laporte has no trouble in establishing that the doctrine of Port-Royal constituted the soul of the *Pensées* at least as much as that of the *Provinciales*.[51] For him, the different reflections of Pascal should be brought under three headings :

1. Presentation of the problem : or an appeal addressed to the conscience of the unbeliever to draw him out of his indifference with respect to religious matters, and to bring him to a search for true religion.

2. Statement of the solution : or an exposition of the Christian religion as the only one capable, through its dogmas and its ethics, of answering the anxiety and the needs awakened in the unbeliever.

3. Demonstration of the solution : or the development of the proofs which make the Christian religion appear not only satisfying to man, but divine and divinely revealed.[52]

Does this plan not constitute, as we have already suggested, the projection into the realm of apologetics of the very experience of Pascal in which the Bible had come to have so much importance? Through these three essential headings, Laporte remarks, such an apology appears to have been taken from Jansenism. And what can this mean save that Jansenist views, strictly Biblical, were dominant in Pascal during the latter part of his life when God took full possession of him? The edition of Port-Royal, moreover, even though it constitutes a Jansenist commentary on Pascal, was eager to attenuate certain passages, or prudently to suppress them in the hope of religious conciliation.

The preface of the Port-Royal edition reported the interview which Pascal had had with these gentlemen toward 1657 or 1659, and in the course of which he had sketched his design.[53] According to Pascal, " The Christian religion has as many signs of certainty and of evidence as the things which are received in this world as the most indubitable."[54] Starting— and this was something quite original—from a picture of man that will arouse the free-thinker who would recognize himself in it, Pascal would have sent his interlocutor to the philosophers, then to the infinite number of religions in the universe and in all ages, to cap the climax. Next he would have presented the Jewish people and the " unique Book by which they are governed, and which comprises their whole history, their laws and their religion." And finally he would have unfolded the story of the fall of man and the redemption in " this same Book," carrier of the Good Tidings.[55] And Pascal would exalt " this Book in which he has discovered the truth," " this same Book " where his interlocutor will find " the means of consoling himself." This exaltation of the

Book knew no limits when one arrived at the fundamental proofs of the Christian religion.[56]

The *Discours sur les Pensées* (written by Filleau de la Chaise) likewise exalted in Pascal "the eloquence, the profundity, the intelligence of what is most hidden in the Scriptures."[57] Did Pascal not also know "how few men have intelligence fitted for metaphysical reasoning"?[58] He was to go through human philosophies in order to raise himself—or to be raised—to a Biblical argumentation. We have insisted enough on the fact that Pascal had quite early turned from scholasticism to attain a theology drawn from the Scriptures. The *Discours sur les Pensées* presents, then, in beautiful order these Biblical themes in which Pascal had recognized himself in the course of the great moments of his experience : the fall, and its consequences; the hidden God, His Book, which reveals man to himself and makes him see clearly the order in the world, the only Book which has revealed to man the true good and which has promised healing. This healing is not in the hand of man; and on this point the Jansenism of the *Discours* is certainly recognizable.[59] The greatest authority for attracting the belief and faith of men is the authority of miracles and of prophecies. By the obscurity of the latter, a hidden God made Himself incomprehensible to evil, and increasingly clearer to those who search for Him. From this observation we understand the two meanings of Scripture, blinding some and enlightening others. Himself enlightened, Pascal would then have shown us how, with the Old Testament serving as a cryptograph of the New, all Scripture leads to Jesus Christ and derives from Him full meaning.[60]

This same insistence on the Bible will be found in the résumé of the *Pensées* by Nicole:[61] "The Plan which M. Pascal had, to restrict himself to the proofs taken either from the knowledge of man, or from the prophecies and from different remarks on the Scriptures, is the reason that one does not find others in his papers; and it is certain that abstract and metaphysical reasoning is quite far removed from this."[62] On this point, *Le Plan d'après Mme Périer* echoes Nicole, since according to Pascal, this kind of proof can lead only to a speculative knowledge of God, and to "know God in that way was not to know Him."[63] And Mme Périer explains at length that the God of Pascal was the Living God of the Bible, "the God of Abraham and of Jacob, the God of the Christians";[64]

that consequently it was necessary " to strive only to know Jesus Christ."[65]

In addition, one finds in the *Pensées* outlines of a plan in Pascal's own handwriting. Fragment 60, for example, presents to us a very simple plan of which the author has thought a moment :

" First part : Misery of man without God.

" Second part : Happiness of man with God.

" In other words :

" First part : That nature is corrupt, the proof being drawn from nature itself.

" Second part : That there is a restorer, the proof being drawn from Scripture."[66]

This plan of the *Vindication* reduced to its simplest expression is very curious. Its purpose is here unquestionable in that it presents with highest evidence the keystone of Pascal's project as being Jesus Christ, the Redeemer according to Scripture.

Here are some résumés of " proofs " of the Christian religion, Fragments 289, 290, which are just so many outlines or searching for ideas.[67] The first fragment gives a central place to " the marvels of Holy Scripture," Jesus Christ, the apostles, Moses and the prophets, the Jewish nation, the permanence of our religion, and " the doctrine which makes everything rational." The second fragment is much briefer : " Ethics—Doctrine—Miracles—Prophecies—Figures."

An examination of Fragments like 642 and 602 reveals that there are three ways of re-establishing unity between the Book of the Jews and the Book of the Christians : (1) The Old Testament has a literal sense and a figurative sense. (2) the Old Testament announced a spiritual Messiah. (3) Jesus Christ was this Messiah.[68]

Ah, certainly Pascal was faithful to the revelation of the *Mémorial*!

From this high place one can measure the profound incomprehension of the optimistic rationalism of the eighteenth century, of Voltaire and of Condorcet with regard to Pascal.[69] " What a chimera is then man? what chaos, what a subject of contradiction! " cries Pascal. And Voltaire comments, " *The true speech of a sick man.*"[70]

In our time, Paul Valéry echoes in his way Voltaire and Condorcet. All three of them regret to see the fine intelligence of Pascal lose itself in religion. They do not realize that it is

" lost " there so as to find itself. Pascal is frightened by the
silence of infinite space. This cry makes the author of
Eupalinos think of " that unendurable barking which the dogs
turn toward the moon."[71]

Valéry does more than renew the Pascalian criticism of the
eighteenth century : he attacks the romantic interpretation
which, in the nineteenth century, made of Pascal " a kind
of French Jansenist Hamlet, who weighs his own skull, skull
of a great geometer, and who shudders and dreams."[72] Henri
Peyre saw very well that the reproach of the highly intelligent
Valéry proceeded from the vast and delicate comprehension
of a humanist. The admirer of Leonardo da Vinci finds the
Jansenist antitheses of Pascal artificial : geometry, finesse;
grandeur, misery; Epictetus, Montaigne.[73] We believe that
we have shown in these pages, however, that Pascal states
antinomies in order to resolve them in a higher order. The
Variation sur une " Pensée " of Valéry is found to offer the
best opportunity possible to study the basic antinomy which
is established behind these debates : that of naturalism and
supernaturalism. The superiority of Pascal lies precisely in
the fact that naturalism is not foreign to him. He traversed
it to attain the higher order. He stated the paradox in order
to solve it by searching in a higher realm for the crux of the
problem. And it was the Scriptures which uncovered this
point to him. Valéry, on the other hand, considers that in the
last analysis the search for the first cause is " an instinct which
may be ascribed to our vertical position,"[74] and that is as it
should be. One must wager, said Pascal.

Every way leads to God provided that one takes the path.
What the Christian layman wanted to obtain in his *Vindication*
was to shake the torpor of the indifferent, to bring him to admit
that God is not an impossibility, that it is only the refusal to
orient oneself toward Him that makes Him appear such. The
nature of the wager[75] of Pascal has been terribly misjudged
by making it a variation on the theme *will to believe* which
the peripheral theory of James and Lange was finally to eluci-
date. The fact is that the argument of the wager, according
to a method familiar to Pascal, catches the free-thinker at his
own gamble and addresses him at first in the only language
he understands, that of " human reasoning."[76] God exists or
He does not. In a domain beyond our reason, there is a game
the meaning of which differs according as to whether God

exists or not. You must take sides on this issue. You must bet. You have no choice. You have already embarked. Keeping your point of view, let us see now what you have to gain or lose, according to whether you wager that God exists or that He does not exist. Now, the rule of probability and of the stakes proves to you—and Pascal establishes it[77]— that by wagering for God, if God does not exist, the player loses after all only a finite value of dubious quality; at the most he takes the risk of merely leading a life that is on the whole noble and advantageous; but in making his wager against God, if God exists, he will lose " an infinity of life infinitely happy " and vice versa. It is the decision for God, the supreme step, that Pascal wants to obtain from the indifferent whom he has just buttonholed; he wants a full and unconditional surrender.

Certainly, the reasoning of Pascal can convince the mind without securing action. Lachelier has definitely shown that what is left to be done is to pass " from the formal absolute to the real and living absolute, from the idea of God to God."[78] But Pascal has well realized—and he is, in this sense only, a precursor of James and Lange—that action greatly overlaps the syllogisms of the intellect. From the moment the recently indifferent consents to live as a Churchgoing Christian, the very act of worship will generate in him the feeling and drive with which it was ordinarily associated, since this act of worship first brought them to life. But more follows—and one cannot dwell on this sufficiently : since God exists, and since the searcher would not look for Him had he not already been found by Him, each step in the new way will give rise to a revelation which will henceforth make his walk firmer and his path easier.

Let us here recall a worthy argument according to which Pascal is said to have owed the idea of his wager to a Jesuit Father whom he had taken to task. However, we must now affirm in conclusion that the first fundamental idea had long since come to him from the Bible : " I call heaven and earth to witness this day, that I have set before you life and death, blessing and cursing. Choose therefore life, that . . . thou . . . may live."[79] And it is to the Bible that Pascal would finally refer the man whom he had just snatched from his gaming table.

In order to estimate to what extent the Biblical apologetics of the *Pensées* is basically in conformity with the real tradition of the Church, it would be well to refer to the admirable work, *L'Art Religieux du XIIIe Siècle en France* of Emile Mâle.[80] The author shows here that since the days of the catacombs Christian art has spoken in type;[81] that the Old Testament appears to the thirteenth-century artist as a prefiguration of the New.[82] Reading from the great Bible of stone, as we might call the medieval cathedrals, Mâle discovers a profound harmony between the Old and New Testaments. And because the synagogue could not read the harmony therein, it is represented in the art of the thirteenth century as a blindfolded figure.[83] As circumstances in our profession have led us to read Pascal and Mâle at the same time, we have wondered many a time whether we were visiting Chartres, or if it were the Biblical structure of the *Pensées* unfolding before our eyes. "The Old Testament has meaning only with respect to the New," wrote Mâle as Pascal had done before him. And then he would add in the same spirit as Pascal : "This doctrine, which has always been that of the Church, is taught in the Gospel in the words of Jesus Himself."[84] Jesus Christ is the meaning and key of all creation, as well to the universe as to man. He is God incarnate, Redeemer and sovereign Master of the new heaven and of a new earth wherein justice will dwell, and through it all is the key to the Bible. This is the *raison d'être* of Pascal's *Pensées*.

Culmination in Christ

Pascal, the Christian layman, wanted to be the John the Baptist of modern times, to prepare the way for Him whose shoe latchet he felt himself unworthy to unfasten. Like John the Baptist, Pascal preached repentance : "One must realize both one's wretchedness and one's unworthiness as well as the need for a mediator." We cannot know Jesus Christ " without knowing at the same time both God and our wretchedness because He is not simply God, but God the healer of our miseries." We must then "strive solely to know Jesus Christ."[85] The whole Scripture culminates in Jesus Christ.[86]

Pascal denounces the Philosophers who think they can attain unto God without Christ.[87] Christ alone is the *Way*, the *Truth*.[88] "Jesus Christ is a God to be approached without pride, and before Whom one is humbled without despair."[89] Pascal summarizes Christ's message in these words : "Jesus Christ did nought but to teach men that they were lovers of themselves, that they were slaves, blind, wretched men and sinners; that He needs must free them, enlighten them, bless and heal them; that that could be done by hating oneself, and by following Him through the suffering and the death of the Cross."[90] Here we have, wonderfully summarized, the Good News, as our Christian layman announced it. Without being irreverent, we permit ourselves to add, addressing ourselves first of all : " Please copy! "

In Jesus Christ is " all our virtue and all our felicity. Aside from Him, there is only vice, wretchedness, wrongdoing, darkness, errors, death, and despair."[91] Through Jesus Christ we know God and " we can know God only through Jesus Christ. Without this Mediator, all communication with God is disrupted. . . . Jesus Christ is therefore the veritable God of men."[92] " Not only do we know God only through Jesus Christ, but only through Jesus Christ do we know ourselves; we know life and death only through Jesus Christ. Outside of Jesus Christ, we know neither what our life is, nor our death, nor God, nor ourselves.

" Thus, without the Scripture, which has only Jesus Christ as its object, we know nothing, and see only darkness and confusion in the nature of God and in nature herself."[93]

Pascal preaches Jesus Christ, and Christ crucified. Nothing can enable us to know and to love God, " except the virtue of the folly of the cross, without wisdom or signs; and not the signs without this virtue."[94] What enables us to believe " is the cross,"[95] and in support of this, Pascal cites a fragment of 1 Corinthians i. 17.

Pascal preaches Jesus Christ, and Him resurrected. In the sepulchre where He was shrouded by the saints, and where they alone could penetrate, Jesus Christ took on a new life— not that of the cross. " This is the last mystery of the Passion and of the Redemption." Living, dead, entombed, resurrected, Jesus teaches.[96]

Blaise Pascal, Christian layman, preaches Christ in His entirety in the *whole* Bible.

Let us leave to the exegetes the concern of knowing how Pascal might have begun his *Vindication*. We already know that he would have wanted it to bear the stamp of Jesus Christ, who would have been its central inspiration, as He is the central inspiration of the Bible, and for the same purpose. We also know how Pascal *came* to write his *Vindication*. As Jesus

Christ had become for him the basis of all things, Pascal, with the simplicity of a child, and often using the very words of the Bible, began to write an *Abrégé de la Vie de Jésus-Christ*.[97] Faugère admits in the *Avant-Propos* of his edition (pp. 13, 14), that Pascal had the idea of publishing this *Vie de Jésus-Christ*, and that he doubtless regarded such a work as the essential introduction to his *Apologie de la Religion*.

In his *Abrégé*, Pascal closely followed the *Series Vitae Jesu Christi* of Jansen; however, he lent to the contents a new emphasis, and he added to the summary of Jansen, by referring to the Biblical texts. He further enriched this historic exposé with commentaries borrowed chiefly from the *Tetrateuchus* of Jansen. But toward the end of his work, he abounded in personal reflections, reminiscent of the *Mystère de Jésus*.[98]

Although the very first part of the preface to the *Abrégé de la Vie de Jésus-Christ* is a commentary on Chapter I of The Gospel According to John, the text is amplified by explanations borrowed for the most part from Saint Paul. For example, the Word is made man " in the fullness of time " (Galatians iv. 4), assuming " the form of a slave " (Philippians ii. 7). He suffered "until death and death on the cross." Pascal does not use quotation marks, nor does he make any Biblical references to preceding lines. Such is his method as a student steeped in the Bible, having assimilated the very marrow and substance of the Holy Book. His style is fashioned by the Bible. Because his thinking is so closely identified with it, he uses Biblical texts unconsciously. Pascal's thought flows naturally into Biblical expression.

We are here dealing with the central message Pascal wanted to express without burdening himself with our present-day scruples concerning quotations and references. That he had a publication in view is indicated in the last paragraph of his preface : " If the reader finds here something good, let him give thanks to God, the only Author of all good. And for what evil he finds, let him pardon my infirmity."[99]

His didactic intention is again marked in the fact that Pascal inserts into his Biblical references dates and events which are not in the Bible itself, but which Jansen had worked out with precision in his *Tetrateuchus*.[100] However, errors slip in here and there:[101] The author writes, for example, " January " instead of " March "; " twenty-six " days after the birth of Christ, instead of " thirty-six." Pascal works between Jansen and his Bible, referring faithfully to the Holy Book according to the indications of his guide.[102]

In regard to this it is interesting to see what use Pascal makes of Scriptural references, as, for example, Luke ii. 41, *seq.*, cited by Jansen. He sums up twelve verses (Luke ii. 41–52) in these few simple and beautiful sentences : " And twelve years later, his parents took Him to the feast at Jerusalem and He stayed in the Temple discussing with the doctors. His parents searched for Him with a great anxiety. He told them that He must accomplish the things His Father had sent Him to do, and having gone back with them, He was subject to them, and grew in wisdom, in years and in grace before God and men."[103]   Luke ii. 41, 42 is thus summed up by Pascal in that twelve years after the birth of Jesus, His parents took Him to the feast in Jerusalem. The fact is that at the age of twelve each Jewish boy became a " son of the Law." As such, he was submitted to a course of studies and trained in fasting and in attendance upon public worship. This is what the parents of Jesus saw from the human viewpoint : that is to say, from the short-sighted viewpoint. But why this eclipse in their memory? Had Joseph forgotten the warning of the angel of the Lord seen in a dream (Matthew i. 20), and Mary, the visitation of the Angel Gabriel (Luke i. 26–38)? Many unbelievers have stumbled on this passage of Luke ii. 43–45. Pascal doubtless saw there only human erring. In his sight, the spectacle is hardly edifying, so he ignores it.

His aim is that of an apologist. That is why, no doubt, he opposes to the legalism of the parents the fact that Jesus stayed in the Temple to *dispute* with the doctors. Let us note the word *dispute*. The Latin text said, " *Audientem illos, et interrogantem*," and M. de Saci translates quite correctly, " Listening to them and interrogating." This method of question and answer was the usual form of rabbinical instruction. But, to an ardent believer like Pascal, Jesus had no need of such a course of study. He knew. He *disputed* with the doctors. In this the contrast between the human infirmity of Jesus' parents and His already omniscient divinity is clearly seen.

To the astonishment of His parents, to the candid question of His mother, to the affliction of people of a stature out of proportion with His, Jesus answers, according to Pascal, by the affirmation of His mission. In his version of the Bible, M. de Saci translated, " Ne saviez-vous pas qu'il faut que je

sois occupé à ce qui regarde le service de mon Père? " (" Did
you not know that I must be *occupied* with what concerns the
service of My Father? ") Pascal's translation is much stronger :
It is a question of things with which Jesus has been *charged*
by His Father, and which must be *accomplished* by Him,
Jesus. He was the One who was to come. Through Him
the prophecies were coming to pass, and we well know to what
extent Pascal could take advantage of such a situation. The
parents of Jesus did not understand at all; and this fact is in
accord with that short-sightedness already pointed out in them.
Thus Pascal passes by verse 50 : " And they understood not the
word that He spoke unto them."

Jesus returned with His parents. This is said simply. It is
the natural order of things. M. de Saci declared that Jesus
was *submissive* to His parents. Pascal is more specific : Jesus
was *subject* to His parents, which implies, not a passive attitude, but the continuation of what must be accomplished
according to the design of God, who ordains and allows for a
short time this subjection to human order in His Son who
was made flesh.

We do not think that we have strained the meaning of the
text in the foregoing analysis. These few exemplary verses
show clearly that Pascal's aim was to vindicate Christianity
in his didactic exposé, and it is not without reason that Molinier
was to incorporate the *Abrégé* in his *Pensées de Pascal*. In its
sources, in its ramifications, this fragment seems to have a real
part in the mellowing of Pascal's last years, which would have
given us a *Vindication of Christianity*. Whereas Jansen is satisfied with some simple references, Pascal cites Scripture at
length, but always to bring out the essence in a message
destined to convince the elect that Jesus was indeed the Son
of God, He that should come. Pascal knows how to keep to
a strictly expository method of the Bible sufficient unto itself.[104]
To him, a simple presentation of Scripture proves to be the
best apologetics possible—truth with which our modern
preachers would do well to imbue themselves.

When we come to the Passion, however, the commentaries
are amplified, and the *Mystère de Jésus* recurs like the leading
theme of a great minor symphony. " ' My God, my God, why
hast Thou forsaken me? ' i.e., Why hast thou abandoned me
to my human infirmity, to the tormenting of my torturers,
without consolation? And He turns to God asking the cause

of this abandonment; therefore [one sees][105] that it is the sin of mankind that He was expiating in His innocent flesh."[106]

Pascal, the committed, does not leave Jesus in the tomb. His Jesus is the Christ, who died for our transgressions, was raised for our justification, and glorified in the bosom of the Heavenly Father, with the glory which He had before the world was. The Jesus Christ of the Pascalian *Abrégé* is not only He that should come, but also He that must return. In the glorious finale of his message, the style of Pascal is inseparable from the divine Book : " And this Kingdom shall be without end, where God shall be all in all."[107] Have we read this in The Epistle of Paul to the Colossians (ch. iii. 11, *seq.*), or was it in the Epistle to the Ephesians (ch. i. 23)? Or could it have been a reminiscence of the " *Cujus regni non erit finis* " of the Nicene Creed?

But why try to analyse this irresistible surge of life bursting forth from the ardent heart of Blaise Pascal? It emerges from primitive Christianity, as did of old the volcanic lava from his native Auvergne.

And behold, it burneth ever!

V. THE GREAT DIVIDE

We know all the virtues, martyrdom, austerities, and all good works are useless outside of the Church, and the communion with the head of the Church who is the Pope.
                                                        —BLAISE PASCAL.

IN a letter dated Toulouse, July 25, 1660, Fermat expressed to Pascal his desire of seeing him in order to greet him and to converse with him for a few days; but as his health was scarcely better than that of Pascal, who was at that time resting in Clermont, he proposed to his friend to do him " the· favour of coming half-way " between Clermont and Toulouse.[1] In his answer, dated August 10, Pascal showed himself touched by the honour which the greatest geometer in Europe was doing him. The real reason he desired to see Fermat, however, was on account of the wit and polish of the latter's conversation, and not his position as a great geometer, for, he explained, " to speak to you frankly of geometry, I find it the highest exercise of the mind, but at the same time, I know it to be so useless that I make little distinction between a man who is only a geometer and one who is a clever artisan. Therefore, I call it the finest trade in the world, but it is only a trade : and I have often said that it is good in order to make the trial but not the use of our strength : so that I should not take two steps for geometry. . . . But now there is in addition this in me, that I am steeped in studies so far from that mentality, that scarcely do I remember that there is any such."[2]

The Only Thing That Counts

Pascal was alluding not only to his project of a *Vindication of Christianity*, but to his Biblical studies and to his diligent efforts toward holiness. Henceforth, the only thing which counts more and more for him is salvation.

As we have stated before, Valéry comments : " He has exaggerated, frightfully and crudely, the opposition of knowledge and of salvation "; he had " found "—an allusion to the assurance which Pascal received from Christ[3]—" but doubtless because he no longer sought."[4] The author of this horrible play on words would have profited by meditating on the principle formulated by Boutroux, addressed, it seems, to every student of Pascal : " Pascal, before writing, knelt down and prayed to the Infinite Being to submit unto Him everything that was in the suppliant, so that His Divine Power might be in accord with the suppliant's abasement. Through such humiliation, Pascal surrendered to inspiration.

" It seems that he who would know a genius so high and so rare in its true essence must follow a similar method."[5] This reverent method, be it noted in passing, allowed Boutroux to write the best book we have on the philosophy of Pascal. The eminent teacher of Bergson[6] had understood these words from the *Discours sur les Passions de l'Amour* : " In a great soul, all is great."[7]

It is as a " passionate thinker "[8] that Pascal seeks for the last word of this problem of salvation which he approaches from the point of view of true conversion.[9] It is also as a utilitarian avid for what is certain, tangible, palpable. It is as a humble penitent who knows that God owes him nothing but chastisement, and that the slightest good received from on high is by pure grace.

The Saintliness of Pascal

This man, so great in all things, became as simple as a child with regard to piety, writes Gilberte[10] of her brother Blaise. Those who saw him regularly were astounded by it. There was in his ways of acting neither affectation nor hypocrisy. He knew how to raise himself to the highest virtues; he knew how to lower himself in the practice of the most everyday virtues which are the edification of piety. All things were great in his heart from the moment that they served to honour God. The curé of Saint-Etienne-du-Mont, who saw him in his last illness, admired that simplicity, and never wearied of repeating : " He is a child; he is humble and submissive like a child."[11]

Pascal masters pleasure; he masters suffering; he reduces almost to nothing the necessities of his poor body. He proscribes comfort, elegance, everything superfluous. The tapestries of his room are useless : he has them taken away. He renounces the pleasures of the mind as those of the senses. To pay attention to food is in his eyes a sensual thing. Neither sauce nor relish; nothing that is destined to excite the appetite. He consumes what is strictly indispensable, after regulating it once for all. He swallows the most repugnant medicines without showing the least disgust. Certainly his life is a *heroic life*, according to a pertinent title of Victor Giraud.[12]

Amiot himself speaks of heroism in connection with Pascal, finds in him its noblest and truest meaning. And since this heroism lasts a lifetime, it is " more beautiful than *Polyeucte*, a play which lasts but a day." There is nothing like it in Saint Catherine of Siena, not even in François de Sales or in Fénelon.[13] It is the heroism of a man who knows that " the last act is bloody, however beautiful the rest of the comedy may be : one casts earth upon his head, and so forever."[14] Such heroism was to wring from bold Pierre Bayle the cry of admiration which has remained famous : " A hundred volumes of sermons are of less value than that life."[15] The principle of that heroism is made manifest with divine simplicity. Beurrier's *Mémoires* sum it up in the affirmation that Pascal had founded " the regulation of his life on evangelical principles," and that " he kept them ceaselessly before his eyes, and tried always to perfect himself more and more in them."[16]

The saintliness of Pascal is henceforth that of a man who hopes for nothing from the world, who fears nothing from it, nor wishes anything from it; of a creature for whom, according to a fine contemporary Russian document, " the final Judge of every dispute is not man, but the One Who holds Himself above man. It results that, in order to find the truth, one must be free from what human beings hold for truth."[17] Such piety, if rigorously consistent, may appear overdone; but as the great Protestant thinker Vinet very well says : " It is good that such vocations, such souls should exist; it is upon such overabundance of spiritual life that the Christianity of the masses is nourished."[18]

The Pascal of the last years knows how to transpose human affections into the divine order. Detached from others, he wishes that they be detached from him. It is to the Creator that he wishes the heart of the creature to be consecrated. Any purely human affection constitutes a turning aside from that which one owes to God. Blaise even goes so far as to discourage by his coldness the attentions of his family. He seeks never to lose consciousness of what he considers an essential duty. The proof of it is that, according to the testimony of his sister Gilberte, there was found on him a little paper, like that he was often seen to read, on which he had written : " It

is unjust that anyone attach himself to me, although he do it
with pleasure, and voluntarily. I shall deceive those in whom
I shall awaken the desire; for I am not the end and aim of anyone, and I have nothing with which to satisfy him. Am I not
about to die? Thus then the object of their attachment will
die. As I should be guilty of creating belief in a falsehood,
even though I should urge it gently, and although therein they
should do me a pleasure; in like manner I am guilty if I make
myself loved, and *if I draw people to me*; for they must
spend their lives and their efforts in drawing near unto God,
or in searching for Him."[19] It is we who have italicized the
passage : *if I draw people to me*, which appears to us, in Pascal,
an assiduous reader of the Bible, as a reminiscence of the " *I
shall draw all men to Me* " of Jesus. There is in this affirmation—take our word for it—the key to the motivating principle of Pascal. We have personally just re-read the Bible from
one end to the other, and what struck us most forcibly was that
the commandment which recurs there most often, in one form
or another, is the " *Thou shalt have no other gods before me* "
of Mount Sinai. Looking closely into the life of Pascal, and
its successive separations, we see there a more and more consecrated observance of this commandment. The last separa-
tion, the hardest, was the detachment from his intimates.
Hence this constant recalling of the little paper always within
reach. Hence the future indicative of an unshakable resolution : *I shall deceive those in whom I shall awaken the desire*
—the desire of attaching oneself to him, Blaise, of making of
him a little god, despoiling all the more the only true God
who will have no other gods before Him.   223984

The preceding interpretation seems to us confirmed by a
fragment of the *Pensées*, where Pascal, in dramatic style,
appears to identify himself with the Old Testament as he
writes : Let those who are of the earth, earthly and given over
to the flesh, become surfeited with it and die in it. " But those
who seek God with all their heart, who have no displeasure
save in being deprived of the sight of Him, who have no desire
save that of possessing Him, and no enemies save those who
turn aside from Him other men, who are afflicted to see themselves surrounded and dominated by such enemies; let them be
consoled. I announce to them good news : there is One come
to liberate them." To others he will not show God.[20] To
make the elect see God, such is his task, according to Scrip-

ture. This task is first of all negative: not to encourage
idolatry. It will be carried out, with this immense reservation
made, by directing his own affections in the way of the elect.
Thus his affections are modelled according to the Bible.

Blaise, his sister Gilberte tells us, had " an extreme tenderness . . . for those whom he believed to belong to God."[21]
This testimony is profoundly moving. Every Christian friendship is founded upon God. It is election in the truest sense of
the word. Matthew Arnold was mistaken when he said that
we are all islands; the novelists and dramatists who erect solitude into a dogma are mistaken. Solitude is for those who do
not know God: and certainly no state is more fertile in
dramatic themes. But the believer sees his solitude peopled
by God's elect, peopled with holy friendships. These friendships, however, ought to be kept in constant reference to God
who is their source and their only reason for being. All the
rest is idolatry and sacrilegious spoliation.

To will what God wills—that is the source of all wisdom.
Pascal was going to write a *Vindication of Christianity*, and
behold the spectre of death standing before him! " Thy will
be done Lord, not my will! " It is for Blaise the supreme test.
He accepts " like a child " the decision of the Father.[22] His
sufferings redouble as the end approaches. Pascal confesses
and accuses himself before God; he lays himself open to the
suffering which purifies; he offers himself to holy pain; he
sinks at the foot of the Cross and consecrates himself there.
The admirable prayer asking of God the effective use of illness,[23] closes thus, the ultimate mystic appeal to the unitary
experience: " Unite Thyself to me; fill Thou me with Thyself
and with Thy Holy Spirit. Enter my heart and my soul, to
bear my sufferings from within, and to continue in me that
part of the suffering of Thy Passion which yet remains to endure, which Thou art yet completing in Thy members until the
perfect consummation of Thy Body; so that, I being filled with
Thee, it is no longer I who live and suffer, but Thou who dost
live and suffer in me, oh my Saviour! and so that thus I may
have some small part in Thy suffering, Thou mayest fill me
wholly with the Glory that it has brought to Thee in which
Glory Thou dost dwell with the Father and the Holy Ghost
for ever and ever. Amen."

In his ardour, Pascal passes unconsciously from involuntary
mortifications to the ascetic penitence of a rebellious flesh. He

who can no longer swallow except with the greatest difficulty not only takes the most repugnant medicines with smiling serenity, but he does not want anyone to feel sorry for him. He does not even want any longer to be cured, saying of the sickness of the body that it is the natural state of Christians. Meanwhile he encircles his bare flesh with an iron belt studded with sharp points—a fact to be discovered only when he was on his deathbed—and he thrusts them into his flesh to remind him of his duty as soon as he feels himself touched by a pleasure to his mind illicit, like that of conversation. Those acts will be recalled after he has uttered his last sigh. " Happy the man who can put a girdle about his conscience," comments Vinet.[24]

Not only does Pascal do " great spiritual exercises in penitence, silence, and the examination or very exact review of his whole life," but he sells all that he can and " gives all the money to the poor."[25] Doubtless these sales multiplied, each time drawing closer to that " total and sweet renunciation." Pascal gives everything. His love for the poor becomes such that he goes so far as to deprive himself of what is strictly necessary. Those about him grow anxious. He repeats gently : " I have noticed one thing. However poor one may be, one always leaves something behind upon dying." He suffers from not having more with which to help the poor, whose eminent dignity strikes him more and more. He sees in them Jesus : " I love poverty, because He loved it. I like wealth because it gives the means whereby to assist the needy."[26] He is persuaded that the spirit of poverty most agreeable to God was to serve the poor in a poor way, by a daily and individual assistance. " To do small things, like big things, because of the majesty of Jesus Christ in us, Who lives our life; and the big things like small and easy ones, because of His omnipotence."[27]

Here are examples of both, if it is permissible for us to speak thus.

Mme Périer reports that three months before Pascal's death, as he was coming home from Church one morning, he was accosted by a beautiful girl of about fifteen who asked him for alms. Struck by the dangers she was running, Pascal confided her to a priest, to whom he gave a purse, promising also to send the next day a woman to buy clothes for the abandoned girl and take care of her—which was done punctually. In spite of the keen desire which he showed at the moment, the

priest did not succeed in finding out the identity of the bene-
factor.

Although great enterprises of charity were not Pascal's particular vocation, we have at least one example of his interest
in such of these as he believed were set aside for God-appointed
individuals.   In 1658, standing on a street corner, he had
noticed that a crowd of people were hurrying in the same
direction.   Why should they not be transported together by
groups?   Pascal had spoken of this to his friend the Duke de
Roannez.   From these meditations was to come the invention
of the omnibus.   But one would misjudge the age in general,
and Pascal in particular, were he to imagine that this invention
was to remain theoretical.   What finally came out of Pascal's
reflections was an omnibus company, conceived with all the
attendant circumstances related thereto.   Saturday, March 18,
1662, vehicles carrying passengers at five sous a ride started
running in the streets of Paris with full pomp and ceremony.
As soon, moreover, as the affair of the omnibuses was arranged,
Pascal asked for a thousand francs in advance on his share, in
order to send them to the poor of Blois, who had suffered
severely from a bitter winter.

Such an insistence on charity on the part of Pascal, as
for the Christians of his century, came, moreover, directly
from the fact that the Vulgate translated the Greek ἀγάπη,
which means *love*, by the Latin *caritas*, which itself means
love, *tenderness*, and became in French, as in English, the
word *charity*.   But *charity* in current speech means : virtue
which causes one to do and to desire the good of others; hence,
to do charity is to give alms.   This meaning is indeed clearly
implied in 1 Corinthians xiii. 1, " If I speak with the tongues
of men, and of angels, and have not *charity* "; but that is a
derived meaning.   In the Greek of the New Testament, the
accent is on *love*.   The passage, " Having *the same charity*,"
of Philippians ii. 2, implies in the Greek text *ardent pursuit*.

This ardent pursuit, in the daily life of Blaise Pascal, is first
of all translated by *alms, help to the poor, to Jesus who suffers
in them*.   " One should have no rest, one should not sleep "
during that time, comments Leo Schestow[28] in a fine page inspired by the " Jesus will be in agony until the end of the
world," of the *Mystère de Jésus*.   Let it be remembered, finally,
that according to Pascal's great page on the three orders, the
order of charity is the supreme, supernatural order.   It is the

only thing necessary[29] where all human contradictions are resolved. It is the " key of the ancient feast " of which Rimbaud
spoke.[30] Pascal becomes part of a noble Christian tradition,
that of the author of the *Imitation of Christ,* for whom the
order of charity is the order of grace : " This *grace* is a supernatural light and a sort of special *gift of God* : it is properly
the distinguishing mark of the elect and the pledge of eternal
salvation."[31] That is doubtless why, in the eyes of Pascal,
charity establishes itself as " the only object of the Scriptures."[32]
Man is free, but he cannot originate in his heart the love of
God. To reach ultimately the order of charity, of grace, means,
therefore, for Pascal that one should have the sign that one's
election is confirmed. That is for him the *supreme implication
of that page on the three Orders, the laborious elaboration of
which we have followed from the first pages of this book.*

We have come henceforth to the final grandeur of Pascal, to
the hour when " the most impatient of geniuses yields to the
saint." Yields? Let us say rather with Charles Du Bos, becomes only an " impetuous tributary of saintliness," in a fusion
of " feeling " and of " vision."[33] In the detachment of saintliness, Pascal has left pleasures " only for others greater," according to the terms of a letter that he wrote several years before
to M. and to Mlle de Roannez, appealing to the testimony of
Saint Paul and Saint John, and interpreting the parable of the
hidden treasure in The Gospel According to Matthew.[34]

After the manner of the Jansenists, and contrary to an
opinion commonly held, Pascal is not sad : he is joyous, even
if his joy appears egotistic to Abbé Bremond.[35] Every thought
of salvation, in a certain sense, can be so qualified; but is it
the fault of the elect if it has pleased God to consider precious
the human soul in particular, and to put salvation on a purely
individual basis? The shadow of La Rochefoucauld hovers
over this type of criticism. Would to God that the " egoism "
of Pascal might spread abroad through the world! It is, moreover, very largely compensated for, it seems, by the charity
of Pascal.

However, the objection of Bremond goes deeper, and is not
lightly to be refuted : While orthodox Catholics say, " Christ
died for all men; He died *also* for me," the Jansenists reason,
" Surely, Christ did not die for all men, but He died for us."
Here the quarrel concerning a proposition attributed to Jansen
is rekindled. If Pascal asks himself the question, it is because

the Bible posed it for him and in the most specific manner. Many fragments of the *Pensées* reveal to us Pascal sounding Scripture on this point.[36] He notes, for example, that Jesus Christ " never condemned without a hearing " (Fr. 780), but suggests that " Jesus Christ, in the quality of the Redeemer, is not perhaps the Master of all " (Fr. 781). It is to be observed that this last fragment is presented in a dialogue form. For this reason, it constitutes, properly speaking, a piece of research, a *skepsis*. Fragment 774 is clearer : it opens with the proposition : " Jesus Christ for all," and ends with the proposition, " It belongs to Jesus Christ to be universal; even the Church offers sacrifice only for the faithful : Jesus Christ offered that of the cross for all."

The Anguish of Pascal

Pascal's joy, we see, is not unmixed, but that comes from the fact that he cannot entirely rest on the message of the Good News such as he finds it in his Bible, and such as the inner testimony of the Holy Spirit enlightens him with respect to it. What do I say? The blessed ambiguity of the Scripture, blessed because so willed by the hidden God, allows him to glimpse a whole divine strategy in which the assurance of his salvation lies in suspense : Am I or am I not called, until the end of my days, to be a part of the small flock of the elect? The notion of the perseverance of the saints does not succeed in taking full possession of him.

The elect will not know their virtues, nor the condemned the greatness of their crimes. " Lord, when did we see Thee hungry, thirsty," et cetera?[37] Faith is not within our power.[38] We must not expect it of ourselves. Quite otherwise, it comes when we expect nothing of ourselves.[39] It is in this sense that Blaise heard Jesus saying to him, " Thy conversion 'tis My concern."[40] Here is truly the anguish of Pascal! A letter to M. and to Mlle de Roannez tells of Pascal's fright at the idea that one may fall from such glory. He appeals to 1 Corinthians ix. 27 : " But I chastise my body, and bring it into subjection : lest perhaps, when I have preached to others, I myself should become a castaway." And he ends on the note of the psalmist (Psalm iii. 1) : " Blessed is the man that feareth the Lord."[41] Another letter specifies that anxieties do not come from the good which is beginning to exist within us, " but from the evil which is still there, and that we must continuously diminish."

Henceforth Pascal prays God to enclose him within his limits, in particular not to let him become involved in the fear of the future : " The present is the only time which is truly ours, and of which we must make use as God wills."[42]   However, does it not appear that Pascal's anxieties come from the past as much as from the future, and in particular from burning memories of his months of backsliding?   Let no one accuse us of appealing too often here to the testimony of the writings from dates as far off as those of 1656 and 1660.   In the words of Jacques Chevalier, if " the whole work " of Pascal moves toward true peace, it does so through a war to be preferred to " false peace."[43]

The question, then, is to discover whether Blaise Pascal ever knew serenity.   On this point a contradiction which we must explain strikes us.   On the one hand, the *heart* in the Pauline sense of the word holds a considerable place in Pascal's thought. For him, faith is " God perceptible to the heart and not to reason."[44]   On the other hand, as far as we ourselves are concerned, we have been able to find in the *Pensées* only two occasions in which specific mention is made of the Holy Spirit.   In Fragment 568, answering the objection that the Scripture is full of things not dictated by the Holy Spirit, Pascal replies that " the Church has never decided " that everything in Scripture was from the Holy Spirit.   Let us note in passing this appeal to the jurisdiction of the Church in the matter.   Pascal adds, moreover : " Even if the Church had decided that everything in Scripture was from the Holy Spirit, that could be maintained."[45]   It would still be the supreme jurisdiction, i.e., the Church, which would be right.   The other allusion to the Holy Spirit is found in Fragment 672 : in the matter of circumcision, Saint Peter and the apostles took into account only " the reception of the Holy Spirit in the person of the uncircumcised "; they did not consult the prophets.   " They judged it to be more sure that God approves of those whom He fills with His spirit. . . . They knew that the end of the law was only the Holy Spirit."[46]   This second allusion shows us again a decision relative to the Holy Spirit, pronounced by Peter and the apostles, that is to say, by the Early Church under the sign of the " chief " of the apostles.   We do not have the right to draw an argument from only two texts—but they are the only ones available.   We shall content ourselves with seeing in them an extremely characteristic symbol.

It is wishful thinking on the part of the Protestant Vinet when he writes : " Let one read the *Pensées* attentively, and then answer this one question : is not Church authority simply a digression in Pascal's system? " The context indicates that he is sure of the reader's acquiescence. How, then, does he come to this conclusion? By identifying purely and simply the *heart* with the Holy Spirit according as it is a question of a " new heart with which the Holy Spirit provides us."[47] Truly one seems to be dreaming in reading this gratuitous transposition of Pascal into Protestant language. The author of this present work does not feel himself authorized to do anything of the sort. In his eyes, it is precisely such operations, which come from sentiments of conciliation praiseworthy in themselves, that have obscured so many similar questions. Let us allow only Pascal, his *Pensées*, his life, to speak. What do we find?

A Matter of Useful Relationship

First of all, the profession of faith of the seventeenth *Provinciale* : " Thanks be to God, I have no bond on earth but to the Apostolic Roman Catholic Church alone, in which I am determined to live and die, and in communion with the Pope, its sovereign head; outside of which, I am fully persuaded, there is no salvation."[48] That is clear enough. In November, 1656, Pascal made a similar profession of faith to M. and to Mlle de Roannez : " We know all the virtues, martyrdom, austerities, and all good works are useless outside of the Church, and the communion with the head of the Church who is the Pope.

" I shall never separate myself from his communion, at least I pray God to grant me this grace; without which I' should be lost for ever. I am making to you a kind of profession of faith, and I do not know why; but I shall neither erase it nor rewrite it."[49] Again a statement which is as clear as it is possible to make it!

May we be permitted to stress this proposition of Pascal that " all the virtues, martyrdom, austerities, and all good works are *useless* outside of the Church, and the communion *with the head of the Church who is the Pope*." Just as we know God only through Jesus Christ, he believes, so we are in a *useful* relationship with Him, as far as our salvation is concerned, only through His terrestrial vicar, who is the Pope. For the

Catholic Church, what is true with regard to Jesus Christ is also true concerning the Holy Spirit. " The Church has authority from God to teach regarding faith and morals, and in her teaching she is preserved from error by the special guidance of the Holy Spirit."[50] " The Saviour took measures that the Church teach us the essential truths without being mistaken and without deceiving us."[51]

It is not to the *testimonium Spiritus Sancti internum* that the Catholic Church appeals : it is to a quality by which the soul is transformed, becomes a child of God; it is on earth the *inchoatio vitae aeternae*. But here is " an essential feature : the faith that Jesus wishes to obtain is not only an individual act; the disciple of Jesus is not an isolated being, he must ' listen to the Church ' (Matthew xviii. 17); the apostles are charged to preach through all the earth, and to baptize all nations; those who refuse to listen to them will be condemned."[52] For the Vatican council invoked by the scholarly Catholic apologist whom we have just cited, " beside the traditional method which seeks for proofs of the divinity of the Christian religion in ' divine deeds,' that is, the miracles and the prophecies, there can exist another, no less legitimate, which comes from the Church as a reality easy to observe and carrying with it the recognizable signs of its divine origin."[53] Pascal, who was so absorbed in the proofs of the Christian religion in the course of the last years of his life, seems to have been affected by this twofold proof.

This duality will prove not to have been foreign to the dualism which was to bring anguish to him as an assiduous reader of the Bible, and as a faithful Roman Catholic. We have seen this anguish reach its climax in an hour of crisis in the cry : " Lord Jesus, I appeal to Thy tribunal! " This antinomy was to be solved by obedience, by submission to the only earthly authority that was competent to judge the debate : the pontifical seat of Rome. Springing from a line of upright men of law, Blaise did not trifle with a matter of competent jurisdiction. Moreover, his own salvation was at stake!

Pascal, says Brunschvicg, remains " the Christian who devoted his whole life to the defence of the true religion and who never had consented ' to be separated from the altar,' to disavow the authority of the Church."[54] With his sister Jacqueline, he could have said : " As long as we do not erect Altar against Altar, as we are not unhappy enough to make a separate Church, as we remain within the limits of simple groaning, and of gentleness with which we endure our persecution, the charity which makes us embrace our enemies will attach us inviolably to the Church." It was a question, for Jacqueline as for Blaise, of not depriving themselves " of the effect of this union."[55] In this notion of an indispensable organic attachment, a condition of life, the parable of the Vine and the Branches is transposed into terms of the Roman Catholic Church and its loyal children. For Pascal it is a question of a " substantial unity from within," of a " sacramental life which assimilates the members to the head."[56] And the " head," of which it is an immediate concern, is for him the visible head, the vicar of Christ on earth, the Pope. In his eyes, the Pope alone disposes of the nourishments of the sacraments which he needs in order to live. This will be seen clearly when death finally takes Blaise by the throat.

For a Catholic like Pascal, it is essentially the sacraments which aid in maintaining the state of grace. Thus their reality, verifiable, evident, and present, becomes precious for the child of Clermont, eager for what is sure, tangible, palpable.

The very subject of the present work might have led us to insist on the Bible to the point of falsifying the perspective of Pascal as a fervent Catholic, anxious to be lacking in none of the practices of his religion. Mme Périer, his sister, tells us that his principal " diversion," especially in the last years of his life when he could no longer work, was to visit the Churches where relics were exposed or where there was some solemnity. To this end he procured an *Almanach Spirituel*, which showed him the places where all the devotions were being held, and which indicated to the faithful the different feasts celebrated in the metropolitan and collegiate Churches, and in the parishes and monasteries of Paris.[57]

In the course of his last weeks, however, Pascal saw scarcely anyone except the curé of Saint-Etienne-du-Mont, who came to visit and confess him. In the month of June, 1662, he had received into his home a family of poor people, one of the children of which had the smallpox. Mme Périer, fearing for her own children, had wanted to have the little sick boy taken elsewhere. Pascal had decided that he himself would be the one to go away. He had therefore abandoned his home to the poor folk and had himself taken to the home of his brother-in-law in the parish of Saint-Etienne-du-Mont. It was thus that he had made the acquaintance of the Abbé Beurrier who henceforth assisted him.

The Grace to Die Well

In this way a great difficulty presented itself, at a time when Pascal felt more than ever that great need of spiritual assistance. The curé of Saint-Etienne scarcely knew him; he did not know the complex events of that great life which was to be so cut short. And then, how many contradictions for that curé whose mind was limited, if not confused![58] M. Pascal did not cease exciting himself against the false Christians who corrupted the Church.[59] Moreover, M. Pascal seemed to blame those of Port-Royal for going too far into the questions of grace. The curé translated: they lacked submission to the Pope. In a deposition dated September 4, 1684, the Duke de Roannez, the faithful friend of Blaise, explains that it was quite the contrary: Pascal meant that the Jansenists by their concessions in the matter of grace, showed too much submission.[60] The Duke specifies that because of his intimate relationship with Pascal he had had "a particular knowledge of his feelings on this matter."[61] It is a fact that his testimony coincides perfectly with that of Pascal concerning the signature of the Formulary —"The only debate worth mentioning which ever set Pascal and Port-Royal against each other," adds Laporte.[62] The Formulary in question was a statement clearly condemning the Jansenist doctrine. In 1661, the Church of Rome required that this Formulary be signed by the clergy and the monastic orders. As the nuns of Port-Royal were profoundly disturbed by the pressure brought to bear upon their consciences, Arnauld devised for them a clever but ambiguous formula to be added to their signature. His phrasing allowed the nuns to preserve their Jansenist faith while paying lip service to the Constitutions. Pascal denounced such expediency as shameful and unworthy of true Christians, in his *Ecrit sur la Signature*, then also in a *Grand Ecrit* which was subsequently destroyed. It was during these debates that Pascal fainted—an incident already recorded in these pages. A short time before, his dear sister Jacqueline had denounced the tyranny of the bishops, saying among other things: " Since the bishops have a courage of maids, the maids should have a courage of bishops." Under coercion she had attained unto the glory of martyrdom: " Unless I see at least a few people make themselves victims of the truth, I must succumb." She had succumbed three months after giving her signature, on October 4, 1661. When a messenger came to bring him the sad tidings, Blaise answered simply : " God give us the grace to die as well as that! "

We may now conclude on this whole unhappy matter of the signature :

There was disagreement with regard to the Formulary, not because Pascal disavowed his former opinions, but, on the contrary, because he found Arnauld and most of the others too moderate. It is a fact that Pascal had continued to go often to Port-Royal. At the end of June, 1662, it was Port-Royal which came to him. Outlawed, and running the risk of arrest, Nicole and M. de Sainte-Marthe succeeded each other at his bedside,[63] where Abbé Beurrier, more and more confused, may have met them. It is to Port-Royal that Mme Périer was to turn in order to publish the *Pensées* of her brother. Laporte concludes his very remarkable study on *Pascal et la Doctrine de Port-Royal* by the assertion that " Pascal does not let himself be separated from Port-Royal."[64] Three letters of 1682, preserved by the *Recueils Guerrier* and signed by Pascal's sister, consider the fact of a supposed recantation by her brother as " a calumny least worthy of belief for all those who knew M. Pascal, and the most false indeed of any that has ever been imagined."[65]

The regrettable controversy had been brought about by the fact that in January, 1665, more than two years after Pascal's death, the former tutor of Louis XIV, Hardouin de Péréfixe, archbishop of Paris, had sent for Abbé Beurrier to ask him why he had granted absolution and the sacraments to a Jansenist as notorious as Pascal. Beurrier justified himself by testifying to the orthodoxy of his parishioner. He added that Pascal had testified that he had retired from the party of Port-Royal because they went too far in the matter of grace and seemed to have less submission than they should for the Pope. Mme Périer and Pascal's friends having protested, Beurrier had formally retracted by a letter of June 12, 1671, to Mme Périer,[66] that we owe to Jansenist sources.

The debate continued from the seventeenth century without new evidence until in 1908 Jovy discovered in the Sainte-Geneviève Library in Paris some unpublished *Mémoires* of Beurrier in which the latter withdrew his own retraction. His penitent, he said in substance, had confessed to him that he had for some time " prudently " retired from the disputes of

Port-Royal, " in view of the great difficulty of those very difficult questions of grace and predestination."[67]   We know,
indeed, that Pascal, after the affair of the Formulary, was to
consecrate the rare hours of leisure which sickness left him to
the preparation of his *Vindication of Christianity*, to prayer, to
reading the Bible, and to charitable works.   What else does
Beurrier say to us?   That Pascal found that these gentlemen
of Port-Royal were going too far in the matter of grace.   Of
the clarification of Beurrier's lack of comprehension on this
subject by the Duke de Roannez, Pascal's intimate friend, we
have already spoken.   Finally, the curé of Saint-Etienne-du-
Mont declares that Pascal had only orthodox sentiments, and
this we have never doubted.   Father Petitot calls attention to
the fact that all the Christians of Port-Royal were orthodox.
Jovy himself published the will of M. de Saint-Gilles, dated
October 5, 1668, where the testator, calling himself " poor
wretch," declares that he has " no other sentiment than those
of my very dear mother the Apostolic Roman Catholic
Church."[68]   Where, then, is the recantation of the Jansenist
Pascal in all that?   In that Pascal probably had a non-Jansenist
end?   Jovy, Strowski, and Jacques Chevalier uphold this, as
well as Abbé Bremond, who introduces nuances and reserva-
tions into his opinion.   For example, there was an evolution in
Jansenism, which cannot be considered as a unit, and decadence
after the bull *Unigenitus*.   The " sect " became schismatic.   Not
so Pascal, who was " only a Catholic like the others."[69]   With
the bull on the table, according to a letter of March 7, 1746,
attributed by Jovy to Father Thomassin, it seemed that there
was only one decision for the Jansenists to make.   Now,
" not one decided for obedience.   The one who most closely
approached it was M. Pascal."[70]

   We shall not pursue any further the study of this controversy, in great part sterile.[71]   In truth, the subject is somewhat repugnant.   Even for a doctor, respect for professional
secrecy is sacred.   What shall we say of the sacred character
for a priest of the confession of a dying man?   The archbishop,
Jovy says, " had promised Beurrier to be silent about his
declaration: he hastened to make that declaration known."[72]
Jovy said neither more nor less than " *the archbishop* "!   It
is difficult for us, after that, to share the emotion with which
the Abbé Bremond, preaching in the cathedral of Clermont
on Sunday, July 8, 1923, for the third centenary of Pascal, cried

out : " In the person of Father Beurrier, it is the whole Church which absolves the dying Pascal, and who recognizes him as hers."[73]

We believe, however, that we have read the essential material on this controversy, and we have integrated it as best we can into what we have already learned of Pascal :

The very concept of election, which is established at the basis of his interests, seems to incite him to seek with even more eagerness for the spiritual nourishment which flows from the organism of the Church through the sacraments. This concept of election is often translated by saying : " I am one of the elect, therefore I persevere." Pascal sees things otherwise. One should rather suppose him to say : " I persevere, therefore I am of the elect." On the subject of grace, he did not change his opinion, but he changed his conduct. Doubtless, if he had been pressed to say what he believed about grace, he would, speak again like Saint-Cyran. Perhaps he would set up the antinomies. But, as Mauriac powerfully expresses it : " He no longer wants to be drawn into this thicket; he has no more time; death is very near; the wind of eternity strikes his face."[74] He hastens away from the land of struggle, throws away his arms and falls on his knees, wishing no more than to suffer and to pray while waiting for the instant fixed by God.

The Pope might have been mistaken, or deceived. What does it matter? What counts is not to have been cut off from the living organism of the Church through which he is nourished by Jesus Christ. What counts is to listen to " those who have the power to remit sins, to consecrate the host, to exile an unworthy man from the Holy Table."[75] The only thing that counts is salvation. It is the Church which disposes of salvation at this last hour. It has the power, at the supreme moment, to cause the crown of election, which is the only wealth for Blaise, to fall from his head.

Already convulsions shake him; already his throat closes. Oh, let the curé hasten to come to give him the viaticum and extreme unction! Yesterday he asked for the Abbé Beurrier several times. In his absence it was M. de Sainte-Marthe who came to spend the night with him. He made his confession. Toward midnight a convulsion shook him from head to foot. Was this, then, the end? And what of the Holy Communion for which he was waiting!

In his night, Blaise saw the holy ciborium shining; his glance

rested on the whiteness of the sacred host where he knew his
Saviour was present in His glory.

"Here is He whom you have so much desired," the curé
announced solemnly.

Blaise, with a superhuman effort of his own strength, half
rose on his bed to receive with more respect the Word incarnate
in spiritual flesh, the Word which was going to communicate
Itself entirely, truly, really, substantially to his soul, to nourish
it with life divine.

But first it was necessary that Blaise answer the questions
on the principal mysteries of faith. And to all the questions
he answered with a holy impatience : " Yes, sir, I believe all
that, and with all my heart! "

And, his eyes bathed in tears, he then received the holy sacrament, extreme unction, and then the benediction of the holy
sacrament : " May God never abandon me! "[76]

These were his last words, the cry of a hope in anguish until
the end, echoing the " May I not fall from Him for ever " of
the *Mémorial*.

For it is in this Catholic context that one must read that burning page of the night of November 23, 1654, and the " submission to Jesus Christ and to my director " in which it
culminated.

Convulsions seized Blaise and did not release him until the
end. He breathed his last August 19, 1662, at one o'clock in
the morning. He was thirty-nine years and two months old.

His funeral rites were celebrated on Monday, August 21, at
ten o'clock in the morning in the Church of Saint-Etienne-du-
Mont.

There were there, around the family, the friends, the sur-
vivors of the former scientific group, the worldly companions,
comrades of combat, converts, and those whom the Christian
layman had helped, writers who had come to pay their tribute
—Corneille, Molière, Bossuet perhaps. At the very back of
the Church and in the aisles the crowds of poor were throng-
ing. Among them were hiding the brothers of Port-Royal,
who feared persecution.

The last liturgical chant having died under the deep vaults,
everyone returned home. The will of Blaise was opened. As
the man of law began to read it, this profession of faith stood
forth : " First, as a good Christian, Catholic, Apostolic, Roman,
the supplicant has recommended and recommends his soul to

God, whom through the merit of the precious blood of our Saviour and Redeemer Jesus Christ may it please Him to pardon his faults and to join his soul, when it shall leave this world, to the number of the blessed, imploring to this end the intercessions of the glorious Virgin Mary and all the saints of paradise."[77]

Let the most strictly evangelical Protestants measure with a glance the abyss which separates them from the most holy, most intelligent, the least scholastic, and the most audacious Catholic student of the Bible, and the most reverent before the Sacred Word who ever lived under God's great sky. Never was a Roman Catholic nearer evangelical Protestantism, nor farther away. In this supreme antinomy is summed up for us the secret of Pascal, and of his anguish.

NOTES

I

1 Giraud, Victor, *La Vie Héroïque de Blaise Pascal*, Les Editions G. Crès et Cie, Paris, 1923, p. 4.

2 Desdevises du Dézert, G., *Pascal et Clermont, Foi et Vie*, No. 13, July 1 and 16, 1923, 26th year, Cahier A., p. 712.   3 *Ibid.*, pp. 711, 712.

4 Pourrat, Henri, *L'Auvergne. Les Limagnes*, B. Arthaud Succr. des Editions J. Rey, Grenoble, 1932, p. 192.

5 Capitan et Peyrony, *L'Humanité Primitive dans la Région des Eyzies*, Stock, Paris, 1924, p. 120.

6 Giraud, Victor, *La Vie Héroïque de Blaise Pascal, op. cit.*, p. 2.

7 Jovy, Ernest, *Etudes Pascaliennes*, Librairie philosophique J. Vrin, v. 7, Paris, 1930 : *Le Grand-Père de Pascal et le Protestantisme*, pp. 217-224. Ernest Jovy's opinion on this point may be accepted without question. The notes appended to his essay include a complete bibliography on the subject. The Catholic author reviews all the facts brought to light by the most recent work of Pascalian erudition, done in the local archives. He concludes : " It no longer appears surprising that, at one period, Calvinism left its mark upon the Pascal home " (p. 224).   8 *Ibid.*, pp. 217-219.

9 This chronology is not yet altogether precise. Victor Giraud (*op. cit.*, p. 8) dates the marriage in " about 1614 "; Régis Crégut, diocesan keeper of the archives of Clermont-Ferrand, says, " About 1615 or 1616 " (*Clermont et les Souvenirs Pascaliens, L'Illustration*, No. 4192, July 7, 1923, p. 2); the same author dates the purchase of the two houses linked by a small courtyard as of 20 February, 1614; Professor Morris Bishop gives 1617 as the date of the marriage (*Pascal, The Life of Genius*, Reynal and Hitchcock, New York, 1936, p. 3). We are following the chronology given by G. Desdevises du Dézert, professor at the University of Clermont-Ferrand (*Pascal et Clermont, op. cit.*, p. 713).

10 In reconstructing this scene, we have borrowed material from the essay by G. Desdevises du Dézert, *Pascal et Clermont, op. cit.*

11 *Gras*, from the Latin *gradus* (step).

12 Crégut, Régis, *Clermont et les Souvenirs Pascaliens, op. cit.*, p. 2.

13 The following entry marks the baptism of Blaise Pascal in the register of baptismal records in the parish of Saint-Pierre, kept since the Revolution at the town hall of Clermont :

" Le vingt-septième jour de juin 1623, a été baptisé Blaise Paschal, fils à noble Estienne Paschal, conseiller eslu pour le roi, en l'Election d'Auvergne, à Clairmont et à noble damoiselle Anthoinette Bégon; le parrin noble Blaise Paschal, conseiller du roi en la Sénéchaussée et siège présidial d'Auvergne audit Clairmont; la marraine dame Anthoinette de Fontfreyde.

" Au registre ont signés Paschal et Fontfreyde.''

14 Chevalier, Jacques, *Pascal*, Plon, Paris, 1922, n. (1), p. 49.

15 *Ibid.*, pp. 48, 49. Fortunat Strowski absolves Pascal from any superstitious practice, adding that he spoke adversely of reason, but that he was consistently and invincibly reasonable, worthy of a disciple of Montaigne (*Pascal et son Temps*, Plon, Paris, 1909-1913, v. 2, 5).

116 THE CLUE TO PASCAL

16 Barrès, Maurice, *Les Enfances de Pascal,* an address delivered at Clermont-Ferrand, in the name of the Académie française, on July 7, 1923, *La Revue Hebdomadaire,* No. 28, 32nd year, July 14, 1923, p. 141.

17 Strowski, Fortunat, *Pascal et son Temps, op. cit.,* v. **2,** 3.

18 Vinet, Alexandre, *Etudes sur Blaise Pascal,* Edition augmentée de fragments inédits publiée avec une préface et des notes par Pierre Kohler, Professeur à l'Université de Berne, Payot et Cⁱᵉ, Lausanne-Genève-Neufchatel-Vevey-Montreux-Berne-Bâle, 1936, p. 3.

19 Why does Fortunat Strowski feel obliged to cast doubt upon this testimony? " I have so often found it misled or misleading," he says in a note [n. 3, p. 8] in *Pascal et son Temps,* v. **2,** *op. cit.*). The Foreword to the new edition [v. **4** to **11**] of the *Œuvres,* **4,** iii, puts the matter more happily : " The precision of Mme Périer [Gilberte] has in almost every case overcome the suspicions of critics who do not recoil from bold hypotheses."

20 Vinet, Alexandre, *Etudes sur Blaise Pascal, op. cit.,* p. 322.

21 Hubert, René, *Les Sciences Sociales dans l'Encyclopédie.* La philosophie de l'histoire et le problème des origines sociales, Alcan, Paris, 1923, p. 29.

22 Desdevises du Dézert, G., *Pascal et Clermont, op. cit.,* pp. 712, 713.

23 Giraud, Victor, *La Vie Héroïque de Blaise Pascal, op. cit.,* p. 21.

24 Stewart, H. F., *The Secret of Pascal,* University Press, Cambridge, 1941, pp. 56, 57.

25 Viscount St. Cyres, *Pascal,* E. P. Dutton and Company, New York, 1910, p. 5.   26 Strowski, Fortunat, *Pascal et son Temps, op. cit.,* v. **2, 8.**

27 Section i, Fr. 10, *Œuvres,* v. **12,** 23.

28 Section i, Fr. 22, *Œuvres,* v. **12,** 33, 34.

29 Strowski, Fortunat, *Pascal et son Temps, op. cit.,* v. **2,** 9.

30 Sa *Vie* par Madame Périer, the manuscript belonging to Faugère in 16°, 82 pp. " Prosper Faugère l'avait acquis de la Bibliothèque d'A.-A. Renouard, qui le tenait lui-même de M. Dequin (1804)." *Œuvres,* v. **1,** 49.

31 We repeat that the version of the Bible cited in these pages for each general reference to the Bible, is that of the Latin Vulgate, first published in English by the English College at Douay, in A.D. 1609, for the Old Testament, and by the English College at Rheims, in A.D. 1582, for the New Testament. Unless special mention is made, our text is taken from the translation published with the approbation of His Eminence James Cardinal Gibbons, Archbishop of Baltimore, John Murphy Company Publishers, Baltimore, Maryland, Printers to the Holy See.   32 *Œuvres,* v. **1,** xlvi.

33 *Pensées,* Section xii, Fr. 793, *Œuvres,* v. **14,** 233.

34 According to Lhermet, it was when the lad began to inquire as to the how and why of things that Etienne Pascal was led to formulate the noted distinction we have described. Lhermet interprets in the sense that Etienne Pascal had in mind " not to separate, but wholly to reconcile faith with reason." His evidence? It appears to be convincing enough for Lhermet : it is that this maxim is in effect a happy condensation of Paragraph I of the *Preface* to the *Catechism of Trent.* This is offered as proof that Etienne Pascal taught his son Church doctrine according to this book, in which the following phrase is indeed found : " The realm of faith begins where the realm of reason ends." In support of this contention, Lhermet cites Pascal's letter to P. Noël, which to him, Lhermet, is nothing other than Thomist in spirit! Furthermore, how does he explain that one of the results of this education was " to divert his inquiring mind from subtle questions of theology "? There are in fact two kinds of theology : positive and scholastic, Lhermet answers. According to him, Pascal was to take up the first, but not the second . . . save in the *Provincial Letters* (Lhermet, J., *Pascal et la Bible,* Librairie J. Vrin, Paris [The title page bears no date, but, on p. 691, the endorsement of the Dean of the

Faculté des Lettres of the University of Paris is dated January 24, 1930],
pp. 22-32).
We have made a special point of adducing for the record these views of a
Catholic writer. In our judgment they err in giving too large a place to
conjecture.
35 Fabre, Lucien, *Pascal et les Sciences, La Revue Hebdomadaire*, No. 28,
op. cit., p. 242.   36 Chevalier, Jacques, *Pascal, op. cit.*, Foreword, p. vi.
37 Bourget, Paul, *Sur Pascal, L'Illustration*, No. 4189, June 16, 1923, p. 595.
38 *Ibid.*, p. 596.
39 Quoted by Fortunat Strowski, *Le Manuscrit des Pensées, L'Illustration*.
No. 4189, June 16, 1923, p. 599.
40 Barrès, Maurice, *Les Enfances de Pascal, op. cit.*, pp. 133, 134.

II

1 Michaut, Gustave, *Les Epoques de la Pensée de Pascal*, 2nd revised and
enlarged ed., Paris, 1902, pp. 1, 2.
2 Barrès, Maurice, *Les Enfances de Blaise Pascal*, in *La Revue Hebdomadaire*,
32nd year, No. 28, July 14, 1923 (Third Centenary of Pascal), p. 134.
3 *Ibid.*, p. 141.
4 On the necessity of the wager, see Pascal's *Pensées*, Section iii, *Œuvres*,
v. **13**, 97-173.
" La question la plus haute de la philosophie, plus religieuse déjà peut-être
que philosophique, est le passage de l'absolu formel à l'absolu réel et vivant,
de l'idée de Dieu à Dieu. Si le syllogisme y échoue, que la foi en coure le
risque; que l'argument ontologique cède la place au pari." J. Lachelier, *Notes
sur le Pari de Pascal*, in *Du Fondement de l'Induction*, 7th ed., Alcan, Paris,
1916, p. 199.
5 *Pensées*, Section vii, Fr. 553, *Le Mystère de Jésus, Œuvres*, v. **13**, 438.
6 Desjardins, Paul, *Pascal Libérateur de l'Intelligence*, in *La Revue Hebdomadaire*, No. 28, 32nd year, July 14, 1923, p. 230.
7 Barrès, Maurice, *op. cit.*, p. 140.
8 Bishop, Morris, *Pascal the Life of Genius, op. cit.*, p. 41.
9 Barrès, M., *op. cit.*, p. 140.
10 Lhermet, J., *Pascal et la Bible, op. cit.*, p. 69   11 *Œuvres*, v. **1**, xlvi.
12 Giraud, Victor, *Pascal l'Homme, l'Œuvre, l'Influence*, pp. 119, 120. Note
further that these notes of a course taught at the University of Fribourg in
Switzerland, date back to 1898, and that the third edition from which we have
taken this quotation dates back to 1905. Since then there has been much
progress in the knowledge of this subject. What interests us here is the
emphasis that an illustrious student of Pascal places on the importance of the
study of the Bible for an understanding of Pascalian thought in its highest
expression.
13 Boutroux, Emile, *Pascal*, Collection *Les Grands Ecrivains de la France*,
10th ed., Hachette, Paris, p. 109.   14 *Œuvres*, v. **12**, lxxxii-lxxxix.
15 *Ibid.*, lxxxii.   16 *Œuvres*, v. **2**, 379, 380.   17 *Œuvres*, v. **1**, 59.
18 *Œuvres*, v. **2**, 90.   19 *Œuvres*, v. **2**, 90, 91.   20 *Œuvres*, v. **2**, 91.
21 *Ibid.*   22 *Œuvres*, v. **2**, 185.   23 *Œuvres*, v. **2**, 92.
24 October-November, 1647. The fragment of a preface to the *Traité du
Vide* is to be found in *Œuvres*, v. **2**, 129-145.   25 Matthew v. 29.
26 Valéry, Paul, *Variation sur une Pensée*, in *La Revue Hebdomadaire*,
No. 28, 32nd year, July 14, 1923, p. 164.   27 *Ibid.*, p. 170.
28 We have borrowed this translation of the descriptive term used by Pascal
from John A. Mackay, *A Preface to Christian Theology*, The Macmillan
Company, New York, 1941, p. 3.

29 *Pensées*, Section vii, Fr. 434, *Œuvres*, v. **13**, 346.
30 *Pensées*, Section vi, Fr. 358, *Œuvres*, v. **13**, 271.
31 *Pensées*, Section vi, Fr. 418, *Œuvres*, v. **13**, 316.
32 *Pensées*, Section vii, Fr. 435, *Œuvres*, v. **13**, 352.
33 *Mémorial de Pascal*, *Œuvres*, v. **12**, 3-7. We have translated three lines from the Latin.
34 *Pensées*, Section vii, Fr. 434, *Œuvres*, v. **13**, 350.   35 *Ibid.*
36 *Pensées*, Section vii, Fr. 434, *Œuvres*, v. **13**, 351. Pascal : *Effundam spiritum meum super omnem carnem* (an exact quotation from Joel ii. 28).
37 *Ibid.* Pascal : *Dixi in corde meo de filiis hominum.* Ecclesiastes iii. 18, an exact quotation. The verse continues in the Vulgate : *Ut probaret eos Deus, et ostenderet similes esse bestiis.*
38 *Pensées*, Section vii, Fr. 435, *Œuvres*, v. **13**, 353, 354.
39 *Ibid.*, p. 353. 40 *Œuvres*, v. **1**, 70, 71. 41 *Œuvres*, v. **1**, 71, n. 3.
42 Lhermet, J., *Pascal et la Bible*, Vrin, Paris, 1930, p. 1. 43 *Ibid.*, p. 56.
44 Testimony of Pascal's elder sister, Gilberte Périer, *Œuvres*, v. **10**, 401.
45 Abbé Bremond, on the other hand, believes that Pascal fainted because of the horror which seized him as he felt the shadow of the Tempter hovering over him at the brink of his own final revolt : " *Le Seigneur ne vient pas à nous dans nos convulsions.*" Bremond, Henri, *Pascal et l'Eglise Catholique*, in *La Revue Hebdomadaire*, No. 28, 32nd year, July 14, 1923, p. 179.
46 " Les Jésuites et leurs adhérents sont les seuls qui croient avoir rencontré ce phénomène, ou plutôt ce monstre, comparable aux hippogriphes et aux licornes. Il n'y a jamais eu de véritables Jansénistes, puisque le premier soin de tous ceux que l'on appelle ainsi est de flétrir avec énergie, comme le faisait déjà en 1657 l'auteur de la XVIIᵉ *Provinciale*, la doctrine décourageante, désolante et impie des cinq propositions dites de Jansénius. Ils protestent en outre de leur passion pour l'orthodoxie et de leur ardent désir de demeurer dans la barque de Pierre, la seule qui puisse arriver au port." Gazier, A., *Histoire Générale du Mouvement Janséniste depuis ses Origines jusqu'à nos Jours*, Champion, Paris, 1923, v. **1**, v.
47 *Pensées*, Section xiv, Fr. 920, *Œuvres*, v. **14**, 343.
48 Jovy, E., *Etudes Pascaliennes*, " Discursions " autour de Pascal, Vrin, Paris, 1928 : D'où vient l' " Ad tuum Domine Jesu, tribunal appello " de Pascal et Saint-Bernard? V. **3**, 85.
49 " Il resterait à déterminer quelles idées Pascal plaçait sous ces mots." *Ibid.*, pp. 85, 86.
50 " Tout au plus velléité passagère de révolte." Henri Bremond adds : " Insensiblement oubliée peut-être, et peut-être aussi, expressément rachetée par une déclaration contraire et les larmes de la pénitence. Cri silencieux de détresse et de confiance, lancé, nous ne savons à quel moment, ni dans quel esprit; intimes colloques avec Celui à qui nous pouvons tout dire; écho résigné à la plainte du Calvaire : *Mon Dieu, pourquoi m'avez-vous abandonné?* En dehors du souverain Juge qui nous comprend mieux que nous ne nous comprenons nous-mêmes, nul ici-bas n'a le droit d'écouter aux dernières portes de l'âme." *Pascal et l'Eglise Catholique*, *La Revue Hebdomadaire*, No. 28, *op. cit.*, p. 175.
51 Sainte-Beuve, *Port-Royal*, 5th ed., v. **5**, p. 177. Quoted in *Œuvres*, v. **14**, 343, n. 3.
52 Mackay, John A., *A Preface to Christian Theology*, The Macmillan Company, New York, 1941, p. 50.
53 *Le Mystère de Jésus*, *Œuvres*, v. **13**, 438, 439. 54 *Ibid.*, 435.

III

1 Ecclesiastes iii. 8; Psalm cxvi. 2; John xii. 34; John xiv. 27; Matthew x. 34.
2 *Pensées*, Section xiv, Fr. 949, *Œuvres*, v. 14, 383.
3 *Le Mystère de Jésus, Pensées*, Section vii, Fr. 553, *Œuvres*, v. 13, 438.
4 *Pensées*, Section vii, Fr. 499, *Œuvres*, v. 13, 399, 400.
5 Psalm cxviii. 27.   6 Psalm cxviii. 9.
7 *Pensées*, Section vii, Fr. 548, *Œuvres*, v. 13, 431.   8 Acts xvii. 11.
9 *Pensées*, Section xi, Fr. 696, *Œuvres*, v. 14, 136. The entire text of the
Fragment is taken from Acts xvii. 11, in the Latin text of the Vulgate. We
shall see that these summaries of selected Bible texts reveal a favourite method
used by Pascal in his study of the Bible.
10 Vallery-Radot, R., *Le Secret de Pascal, La Revue Hebdomadaire*, No. 28,
32nd year, July 14, 1923, p. 204.
11 Cf., for example: *Introduction aux Pensées de Pascal*, *Œuvres*, v. 12,
lxviii; Jovy, E., *Etudes Pascaliennes*, v. 2, 3, Vrin, Paris, 1927; v. 8, 164,
Vrin, Paris, 1932; Mauriac, F., *Blaise Pascal et sa Sœur Jacqueline*, Hachette,
Paris, 1931, p. 193; Strowski, F., *Pascal et son Temps, op. cit.*, v. 3, 302ff.
12 *Pensées*, Section xii, Fr. 744, *Œuvres*, v. 14, 200, 201.
13 *Œuvres*, v. 14, 201, n. 7.
14 *Introduction aux* Pensées *de Pascal*, *Œuvres*, v. 12, cxxxii, cxxxiii.
15 Höffding, H., *Pascal et Kierkegaard, Revue de Métaphysique et de Morale*,
30th year, No. 2, April-June, 1923, p. 221.
16 Quoted by Höffding, *op. cit.*, p. 229.
17 Kierkegaard, S., *Purity of Heart Is to Will One Thing*, translated from the
Danish by Douglas V. Steere, Harpers, New York and London, 1938.
18 Vinet, A., *Etudes sur Blaise Pascal*, ed. Kohler, 1936, *op. cit.*, p. 133.
19 Chevalier, J., *La Méthode de Connaître d'après Pascal, Revue de Métaphysique et de Morale, op. cit.*, p. 193.
     Vid. *Pensées*, Section iv, Fr. 265, *Œuvres*, v. 13, 194, 195; Fr. 273, *ibid.*,
199; Section vii, Fr. 430, *ibid.*, 335, 336.
20 Cf., for example, 1 Corinthians xiii. 12, and Pascal's statement: " Par la
gloire nous connaîtrons sa nature."
21 *Pensées*, Section ix, Fr. 601, *Œuvres*, v. 14, 40.
22 *Pensées*, Section xi, Fr. 700, *Œuvres*, v. 14, 137.
23 *Pensées*, Section xi, Fr. 701, *Œuvres*, v. 14, 138.
24 *Pensées*, Section xi, Fr. 708, *Œuvres*, v. 14, 141.
25 *Pensées*, Section xii, Fr. 787, *Œuvres*, v. 14, 227.   26 Isaiah viii. 14.
27 *Pensées*, Section xii, Fr. 795, *Œuvres*, v. 14, 234, 235.
28 *Pensées*, Section xiv, Fr. 862, *Œuvres*, v. 14, 303-307. The entire Fragment is deserving of careful study from this point of view.
29 *Pensées*, Section xii, Fr. 776, *Œuvres*, v. 14, 219.
30 *Pensées*, Section x, Fr. 684, *Œuvres*, v. 14, 122.
31 Baruzi, J., *Pascal et la " Vanité de la Peinture," La Revue Hebdomadaire*,
No. 28, 32nd year, July 14, 1923, p. 267.
32 *Abrégé de la Vie de Jésus-Christ, Œuvres*, v. 11, 6ff.
33 *Pensées*, Section x, Fr. 684, *Œuvres*, v. 14, 122.
34 *Pensées*, Section ix, Fr. 622, *Œuvres*, v. 14, 65, 66. Cf. also p. 65, n. 2.
35 *Pensées*, Section ix, Fr. 624, *Œuvres*, v. 14, 66.
36 *Pensées*, Section ix, Fr. 625, *Œuvres*, v. 14, 67.
37 *Pensées*, Section ix, Fr. 628, *Œuvres*, v. 14, 69.
38 *Pensées*, Section ix, Fr. 629, *Œuvres*, v. 14, 71.
39 Isaiah xxx. 8; *Pensées*, Section ix, Fr. 630, *Œuvres*, v. 14, 72.
40 *Pensées*, Section ix, Fr. 631, *Œuvres*, v. 14, 72.

41 *Pensées*, Section xii, Fr. 743, *Œuvres*, v. 14, 200.
42 *Pensées*, Section xii, Fr. 737, *Œuvres*, v. 14, 196, 197.
43 *Pensées*, Section x, Fr. 687, *Œuvres*, v. 14, 125.
44 *Pensées*, Section x, Fr. 691, *Œuvres*, v. 14, 129
45 *Pensées*, Section x, Fr. 662, *Œuvres*, v. 14, 98, 99.
46 *Pensées*, Section x, Fr. 648, *Œuvres*, v. 14, 89
47 *Pensées*, Section x, Fr. 649, *Œuvres*, v. 14, *ibid.*
48 *Ibid.*, Fr. 650.   49 *Pensées*, Section x, Fr. 651, *Œuvres*, v. 14, 90, 91.
50 *Préface de Port-Royal*, *Œuvres*, v. 12, cxcii, cxciii.
51 *Pensées*, Section xii, Fr. 797, *Œuvres*, v. 14, 235.
52 *Pensées*, Section xii, Fr. 801, *Œuvres*, v. 14, 238, 239.
53 *Pensées*, Section xii, Fr. 802, *Œuvres*, v. 14, 239.   54 *Ibid.*
55 *Pensées*, Section xii, Fr. 799, *Œuvres*, v. 14, 237.
56 Lhermet, J., *Pascal et la Bible, op. cit.*, pp. 224, 225.
57 *Biblia Polyglotta Vulgo Dicta Vatabli* : ex officina Sant' Andreana, Heidelberg, 1586 (2nd ed., Heidelberg, 1593).

Pascal seems also (cf., for example, Fr. 819 of *Pensées*) to have used the edition given by Robert Estienne in Paris in 1545 and re-edited in Geneva in 1547. This edition provided the text from the Vulgate on the one hand, and on the other a new translation worked out from the original Hebrew. The latter, moreover, was a combination of the translation of Léon de Juda (Tigurina) and that of Sante Pagnino. Also there appeared in 1564 in Bâle an excellent edition of the notes of Vatable and Sante Pagnino, entitled *Biblia Veteris ac Novi Testamenti*. Finally, Robert Estienne incorporated the corrections of Vatable to the Hebrew Bible of Kimchi, 1539-1543, 3 v. Thus Estienne summed up what Vatable had gathered from various commentators, adding to it the benefits of his own strong erudite mind, and what Estienne himself had to say in the form of personal commentaries of Calvinistic inspiration.

An excellent revised and enlarged edition of Vatable was published in Paris in 1745, namely, *Biblia sacra, cum universis Franc. Vatabli, Regii Hebraicae Linguae quondam Professoris, et varium interpretum, annotationibus. Latina interpretatio duplex est: altera vetus, altera nova. Parisiis. MDCCXLV.*
58 Lhermet, J., *Pascal et la Bible, op. cit.*, p. 212.
59 *Ibid.*, pp. 215, 216.
60 Dedieu, J., *Note sur Pascal Traducteur de la Bible*, in *Revue d'Histoire Littéraire de la France*, 40th year, 1933, pp. 80-90.   61 *Ibid.*, p. 81.
62 *Ibid.*, pp. 81-84.   63 *Ibid.*, p. 84.   64 *Ibid.*, p. 90.
65 Mauriac, F., *Pascal et sa Sœur Jacqueline, op. cit.*, p. 193.
66 *Pensées*, Section xiv, Fr. 899, *Œuvres*, v. 14, 329.
67 Strowski, F., *Pascal et son Temps, op. cit.*, v. 2, pp. 355, 356.
68 *Ibid.*, n. 1, 356.
69 Jovy, E., *Pascal et la Bible*, in *Etudes Pascaliennes*, v. 8, Vrin, Paris, 1932, n. 1, pp. 153-155.
70 *La Bible* qui est toute la Saincte Escriture du vieil et du nouveau Testament, autrement l'Ancienne et la Nouvelle Alliance, le tout revu et conféré sur les textes Hébrieux et Grec par les pasteurs et professeurs de l'église de Genève, avec les tables nécessaires pour le soulagement du Lecteur, Saumur, 1614, 2 v., 460 + 138 (sans compter 31 pages non numérotées, d'index et de tables), in 4°.
71 Jovy, E., *Pascal et la Bible*, in *Etudes Pascaliennes, op. cit.*, v. 8, p. 153.
72 Benoist, R., *La Sainte Bible* contenant le Vieil et le Nouveau Testament traduite en françois in folio, Paris, 1566. Another edition in 2 v. in 4° was published in 1568.
73 In regard to this, see especially *Pensées*, Section vii, Fr. 446, and the notes in *Œuvres*, v. 13, 359-363.

74 Cf. *Œuvres*, v. **10**, 55, 56, and n. 1. In regard to the manuscript distribution of books long before formulated, cf. *Œuvres*, v. **6**, 215, n. 3.
75 Daniel xi. 8; Isaiah xlviii; Isaiah lxv. 3.   76 Daniel ii. 27-46.
77 Antoniadis, S., *Pascal Traducteur de la Bible*, Brill, Leyde, 1930, p. xii.
78 *Pensées*, Section xi, Fr. 722, *Œuvres*, v. **14**, 169, 170.
79 *Pensées*, Section x, Fr. 692, *Œuvres*, v. **14**, 131.
80 *Pensées*, Section ix, Fr. 636, *Œuvres*, v. **14**, 79.
81 *Pensées*, Section x, Fr. 661, *Œuvres*, v. **14**, 98.
82 *Pensées*, Section x, Fr. 668, *Œuvres*, v. **14**, 102, 103.
83 *Pensées*, Section x, Fr. 676, *Œuvres*, v. **14**, 112.
84 *Pensées*, Section xi, Fr. 698, *Œuvres*, v. **14**, 136.
85 *Pensées*, Section x, Fr. 682, *Œuvres*, v. **14**, 116-120.
86 *Pensées*, Section xii, Fr. 782, *Œuvres*, v. **14**, 224.
87 Dedieu, J., *op. cit.*, pp. 80, 81.
88 Du Bos, Ch., *Le Langage de Pascal*, in *La Revue Hebdomadaire*, No. 28, 32nd year, July 14, 1923, p. 257.
89 Havet, E., *Etude sur les Pensées de Pascal*, in ed. of *Pensées*, Delagrave, Paris, 1887, p. xxxix.
90 *Pensées*, Section x, Fr. 670, *Œuvres*, v. **14**, 104, 105.
91 Amiot, Ch.-G., *Impressions sur Pascal Romantique et Classique*, in *La Revue Hebdomadaire*, *op. cit.*, pp. 299, 300.
92 Stewart, H. F., *The Secret of Pascal*, the University Press, Cambridge, 1941, pp. 80, 86, 87.
93 *Pensées*, Section vii, Fr. 430, *Œuvres*, v. **13**, 337.

IV

1 Faugère, A., *Le Mouvement Religieux dans la Littérature du XVIIᵉ Siècle*, Boivin, Paris, 1938, p. vi.   2 Cf. *Œuvres*, v. **9**, 234.
3 " The love of truth . . . was always the dominating passion of M. Pascal," writes Dom Clemencet, in § I of his *Vie Inédite de Pascal*, quoted by Jovy, E., *Etudes Pascaliennes*, *op. cit.*, v. **6**, 8.
4 Amiot, Ch.-G., *Impressions sur Pascal Romantique et Classique*, in *La Revue Hebdomadaire*, No. 28, 32nd year, July 14, 1923, p. 304.
5 *Pensées*, Section vii, Fr. 531, *Œuvres*, v. **13**, 421, 422.
6 We are taking here in its spiritual sense an expression borrowed from Fragment 923 of Section xiv of the *Pensées*, *Œuvres*, v. **14**, 352.
7 Cousin, V. *Rapport à l'Académie Française* on the necessity of a new edition of the *Pensées* of Pascal, read at the meetings of April 1, May 1, June 1, July 1, and August 1, 1842, part two, in *Des Pensées de Pascal*, Ladrange, Paris, 1844, p. 115.
8 Cf. *Pensées*, Section iv, Fr. 248, *Œuvres*, v. **13**, 181, 182.
9 Smith, W. M., *The Supernaturalness of Christ*, W. A. Wilde Co., Boston, Mass., 1941, p. vii.
   We warmly recommend this work, whose greatest merit, as we see it, lies in pointing out that the best way to combat naturalism is to bring out the value of supernaturalism in its purest form, i.e., the supernaturalism of Christ. One destroys only that which one replaces.
   These views do not invalidate in any way what is well founded of a naturalism which consents to keep to its place. Pascal has expressed his ideas on this matter in the unforgettable terms of his fragment of a preface to the *Traité du Vide*, *Œuvres*, v. **2**, 129-145.
10 *Œuvres*, v. **12**, cxxxvi.   11 *Ibid.*, ccxlvi.   12 *Œuvres*, v. **1**, 71.
13 Rauh, F., *La Philosophie de Pascal*, in *Revue de Métaphysique et de Morale*, 30th year, No. 2, April-June, 1923, p. 307.

This article was published for the first time in No. 2 of the *Annales de l'Université de Bordeaux* (ed. E. Leroux).

14 Hervier, M., *L'Utilité Pédagogique de Pascal, Revue Pédagogique*, 1923, 2nd sem., p. 85.

15 Fragment *De l'Art de Persuader, Œuvres*, v. **9**, 271-273.

16 *Comparaison des Chrétiens des Premiers Temps avec ceux d'Aujourd'hui,* work not dated, published for the first time in the edition of the Abbé Bossut, 1779, v. **2**, 510. This title has been generally accepted since Bossut. The text of this document will be found in *Œuvres*, v. **10**, 411-418. The quotation which we have just given is found on p. 416.

17 Boutroux, E., *Socrate, Fondateur de la Science Morale*, in *Etudes d'Histoire de la Philosophie*, Paris, Alcan, 1897 (quoted by Giraud, V., *Pascal, l'Homme, l'Œuvre, l'Influence*, notes for a course given at the University of Fribourg, Switzerland, during the first semester of 1898, 3rd edition, revised, corrected, and considerably enlarged, Fontemoing, Paris, 1905, pp. 170, 171).

18 *Sur la Conversion du Pécheur, Œuvres*, v. **10**, 422-426. See in particular, a reminiscence of Matthew v. 19, on p. 424.

19 *Introduction à la Seconde Série des* Œuvres *de Pascal* [v. **4-11**], *Œuvres*, v. **4**, xxv.   20 *Œuvres*, v. **9**, 317ff.

21 *Œuvres*, v. **10**, 156. The quotations are from John vii. 25, and 1 Thessalonians v. 15-18.   22 *Œuvres*, v. **10**, 46.

23 Boettner, L., *The Reformed Doctrine of Predestination*, 5th ed. Wm. B. Eerdmans Publishing Co., 1941, p. 330. The essential defect of this useful work is that too many quotations are given second-hand.

24 *Œuvres*, v. **2**, 537ff.

25 Sabatier, A., *L'Apôtre Paul*, Sketch of a history of his thought, 4th ed. revised and enlarged, Fischbacher, Paris, 1912, p. 350.

26 *Œuvres*, v. **9**, 361.

27 See, for example, his letter to his niece Jacqueline Périer, *Œuvres*, v. **9**, 317ff.

28 *Extrait d'une Lettre de Pascal à M. et à Mlle de Roannez, Œuvres*, v. **6**, 159.

29 See, for example, another letter of November, 1656[?], *Œuvres*, v. **6**, 216, 217, n. 4, 217 (and also n. 1, 215); a letter of the 24[?] of December, 1656, *Œuvres*, v. **6**, 300, 301.

30 Chamaillard, E., *Pascal Mondain et Amoureux*, Les Presses Universitaires de France, Paris, 1923, pp. 436-441. See also the exhortation of Chamaillard to those whom his book would not have convinced, *ibid.*, p. 455.

31 Mauriac, F., *The Living Thoughts of Blaise Pascal*, Longmans, Green & Co., New York, Toronto, 1940, pp. 223, 224.

32 Cousin, V., Unpublished fragment of Pascal *Sur l'Amour*, article in the *Revue des Deux Mondes*, September 15, 1843, reproduced in appendix no. 11, *Des Pensees de Blaise Pascal*, new edition, revised and enlarged, Ladrange, Paris, 1844, pp. 408 and 412.

33 *Extrait d'une Lettre de Pascal à M. et à Mlle de Roannez*, November 5, 1656, *Œuvres*, v. **6**, 159 (see also Fr. 668 of the *Pensées*).

34 Letter of November 5, 1656, *cit.*, 160.   35 *Ibid.*, 161.

36 Cf. *Œuvres*, v. **5**, 402.

37 Cf. Calvet, J., *Pascal Directeur de Conscience*, in *Revue du Clergé Français*, June 15, 1901, for a more strictly Catholic presentation of certain aspects of the subject that we are treating in this chapter.

38 Cf. *Discours sur les Pensées de M. Pascal où l'on essaie de faire voir quel était son Dessein, Œuvres*, v. **12**, cxcix-ccxxxviii. This *Discours* appeared in 1672, under the name of Dubois de la Cour. (Cf. Sainte-Beuve, *Port-Royal*, 5th ed., v. **3**, 386.) See also Filleau de la Chaise, *Qu'il y a des Démonstrations*

d'une Autre Espèce et aussi Certaines que celles de la Géométrie, reproduced in the *Revue de Métaphysique et de Morale*, 30th year, No. 2, April-June, 1923, pp. 215-220. This little treatise, reproduced from the text of the *Pensées de M. Pascal* published by Desprez et Desessartz in Paris, in 1715, is commonly attributed to Filleau de la Chaise, and is found added in most editions of the *Pensées*, to the two other *Discours* put under the name of Dubois, but which are very probably the work of Filleau. In an article of the *Revue Bleue*, January 21, 1922, Victor Giraud showed that this must be the echo of a conversation of Pascal's. In n. 1, p. 205 of *La Vie Héroïque de Blaise Pascal, op. cit.*, p. 257, the same author casts doubt upon the testimony which Etienne Périer is the only one to give, according to which the discourse of Pascal was " made thus on the spur of the moment, without having been premeditated or worked out." The *Discours* of Filleau de la Chaise are to be completed by the *Résumé des " Pensées " par Nicole (Traité de l'Education d'un Prince*, second part, xli-xliii), reproduced in *Œuvres*, v. **12**, ccxxxix-ccxli, and the *Plan de l'Apologie d'après Mme Périer* (Extract of Dr. Besoigne, *Histoire de l'Abbaye de Port-Royal*, v. **4** 469), reproduced in *Œuvres*, v. **12**, ccxli-ccxlvi. All these data are arranged by Brunschvicg in his *Argument Logique des Pensées* for the classification of his edition, *Œuvres*, v. **12**, cclv-cclxxiii. For the comparison of his arrangement of the *Pensées* with that of the manuscripts and the other important editions, Brunschvicg has established an admirable *Table de Concordance, Œuvres*, v. **12**, cclxxvi-ccciv.

39 *Première Lettre Circulaire Relative à la Cycloïde* (June, 1658), *Œuvres*, v. **7**, 337ff.; *Seconde Lettre . . .* (July, 1658), *Œuvres*, v. **8**, 15ff.; *Troisième Lettre . . .* (October 7 and 9, 1658), *Œuvres*, v. **8**, 155ff.; *Histoire de la Roulette* (October 10, 1658), *Œuvres*, v. **8**, 179ff.; *Suite de l'Histoire de la Roulette* (December 12, 1658), *Œuvres*, v. **8**, 280ff.; *Récit de l'Examen et du Jugement des Escrits Envoyés pour les Prix*, November 25, 1658, *Œuvres*, v. **8**, 231ff. See also the letters published in *Œuvres*, v. **8**, 247ff.; 321ff.; 325ff.
40 *Œuvres*, v. **12**, iii-xl.
41 Stewart, H. F., *Vers une Nouvelle Edition de l'Apologie de Pascal, French Quarterly*, September 1921, 132-151. Quoted by Peyre, H., *Pascal et la Critique Contemporaine, The Romanic Review*, No. 4, October-December, 1930, v. **21**, 329. See n. 38 above.
42 *Le Plan de l'Apologie, Œuvres*, v. **12**, liii, liv.
43 Stewart, H. F., *Holiness of Pascal*, Cambridge University Press, 1915.
44 Strowski, F., in his " Edition Définitive " of all Pascal, Ollendorff, Paris, 1923; and the following in their respective arrangement of the *Pensées*: Chevalier, J., Galba, Paris, 1925 (*Nouvelle Revue Française*, Paris, 1937); Massis, G., A la Cité des Livres, Paris, 1929; Dedieu, J., Librairie de l'Ecole, Paris, 1937; Tourneur, Z., Editions de Cluny, Paris, 1938.
45 Stewart, H. F., *Pascal's Apology for Religion Extracted from the* Pensées, Cambridge University Press, 1942.
46 *Pensées*, Section iii, Fr. 185, *Œuvres*, v. **13**, 97.
47 See for example *Pensées*, Section xiv, especially Frs. 902-958.
48 *Pensées*, Section vi, Fr. 370, *Œuvres*, v. **13**, 282, 283.
49 Strowski, F., *Psychologie et Accidents des Manuscrits de Pascal*, in *Comoedia*, 20th year, No. 5,108, Saturday, December 25, 1926. We owe the possession of this rare number, as well as that of the precious number of the tricentenary of Pascal of *La Revue Hebdomadaire*, to the kindness of our friend André Ferrier, founder and director of the Théâtre d'Art of San Francisco. May he find here the expression of our gratitude.
50 Pourtalès, G. de, *Les Editions Originales des " Pensées," La Revue Hebdomadaire*, No. 28, 32nd year, July 14, 1923, 278-286.
51 Laporte, J., *Pascal et la Doctrine de Port-Royal, Revue de Métaphysique et*

de Morale, 30th year, No. 2, April-June, 1923, 265.   52 *Ibid.*, 267.
53 *Préface de l'Edition de Port-Royal, Œuvres*, v. **12**, clxxxii.
54 *Ibid.*, clxxxiii.   55 *Ibid.*, clxxxiv.   56 *Ibid.*, clxxxv-clxxxvii.
57 *Discours sur les Pensées, Œuvres*, v. **12**, cciii.   Compare with the eulogy
of M. Tillemont, v. **12**, ccxlix (Letter of M. de Tillemont to M. Périer, the
son).   58 *Ibid.*, v. **12**, cciii.   59 *Ibid.*, v. **12**, ccxiv.
60 *Ibid.*, v. **12**, ccxxiii-ccxxxi.   Note the considerable place given to Jesus
Christ.
61 *Résumé des " Pensées " par Nicole, Œuvres*, v. **12**, ccxxxix, ccxl.
62 *Ibid.*, ccxli.   63 *Plan d'après Mme Périer, Œuvres*, v. **12**, ccliii.
64 *Ibid.*, v. **12**, ccliv.   65 *Ibid.*, v. **12**, cclv.
66 *Pensées*, Section ii, Fr. 60, *Œuvres*, v. **12**, 61.
67 *Pensées*, Section iv, Fr. 289, 290, *Œuvres*, v. **13**, 210, 211.
68 *Le Classement des " Pensées," Œuvres*, v. **12**, lix.
69 Let us recall in particular the work of Waterman, M., *Voltaire, Pascal and
Human Destiny*, Kings Crown Press, New York, 1942, which sheds light on
the question, with a great indulgence for Voltaire.   We are pleased to render
homage to this effort at comprehension.
70 *Pensées de Pascal* with the notes of M. de Voltaire, Geneva, 1778, v. **2**,
127, 128.
71 Valéry, P., *Variation sur une " Pensée,"* in *La Revue Hebdomadaire*,
No. 28, 32nd year, July 14, 1923, p. 163 (art. reproduced in *Variété*, N. R. F.,
Paris, 1924, pp. 137-154).   Jovy discusses the *Variation* of Valéry in his *Investigations Péripascaliennes*, Vrin, Paris, 1928, v. **4**, 43: *A propos d'une
" Pensée " de Pascal*.   72 *Op. cit., La Revue Hebdomadaire*, 164, 165.
73 Peyre, H., *Pascal et la Critique Contemporaine, The Romanic Review*,
No. 4, October-December, 1930, v. **21**, 335   74 Valéry, P., *op. cit.*, p. 165.
75 Pascal had many precursors in his argument of the bet: Arnobe (*Adversus
Nationes*, I, 53; II, 4); Saint Augustine (*De Utilitate Credendi*, 12, 26); Ray-
mond Sebonde, *Theologie Naturelle*, trans. by Montaigne (ch. 68); et cetera.
76 *Pensées*, Section iii, Fr. 233, *Œuvres*, v. **13**, 145.
77 *Ibid.*, v. **13**, 147-151.   See the important notes of Brunschvicg.
78 Lachelier, J., in *Du Fondement de l'Induction*, 7th edition, Alcan, Paris,
1916, *Notes sur le Pari de Pascal* (175-208), p. 199.   The *Notes* of Lachelier had
for its immediate cause an article of Dugas and Riquier, which appeared in the
Revue Philosophique, September, 1900.   Dugas answered in the *Revue Occi-
dentale*, September, 1901 (*Le Pari de Pascal sur Dieu*).   See the long note
(*Appendice* for Fr. 233) in *Œuvres*, v. **13**, 161-173.   For the recent fate of the
Pari in France, cf. Eastwood, D. M., *The Revival of Pascal, A Study of His
Relation to Modern French Thought*, Oxford University Press, 1936, pp. 84-86.
79 Deuteronomy xxx. 19.
80 Mâle, E., *L'Art Religieux du XIIIe Siècle en France*, Etude sur l'icono-
graphie du Moyen Age et sur ses sources d'inspiration, new edition, revised and
corrected, illustrated with 127 figures, Colin, Paris, 1902.
81 *Ibid.*, p. 28ff.   82 *Ibid.*, p. 162ff.   83 *Ibid.*, p. 163.
84 *Ibid.*, p. 163.   Mâle supports his statement by quoting John iii. 14,
Matthew, xii. 40.
85 *Vie par Mme Périer, Œuvres*, v. **1**, 77-79.
86 Cf. *Pensées*, Frs. 699, 705, 706, 707, 741, 762.
87 *Pensées*, Section vii, Fr. 463, *Œuvres*, v. **13**, 373.
88 *Pensées*, Section vii, Fr. 466, *Œuvres*, v. **13**, 376.
89 *Pensées*, Section vii, Fr. 528, *Œuvres*, v. **13**, 420.
90 *Pensées*, Section vii, Fr. 545, *Œuvres*, v. **13**, 428, 429.
91 *Pensées*, Section vii, Fr. 546, *Œuvres*, v. **13**, 429.
92 *Pensées*, Section vii, Fr. 547, *Œuvres*, v. **13**, 429, 430.

93 *Pensées*, Section vii, Fr. 548, *Œuvres*, v. **13**, 431.
94 *Pensées*, Section viii, Fr. 587, *Œuvres*, v. **14**, 29.
95 *Pensées*, Section viii, Fr. 588, *Œuvres*, v. **14**, 30.
96 *Pensées*, Section vii, Fr. 552, *Œuvres*, v. **13**, 533, 534.
97 *Abrégé de la Vie de Jésus-Christ*, *Œuvres*, v. **11**, 1-94.
This work was published for the first time with much care in the *Revue Ecclésiastique* of September, 1845, v. **88**, 97-134; then edited for the second time by Faugère, published by Andrieux, Paris, 1846 (reprinted in *Pensées*, Leroux, Paris, 1807, v. **2**, 445). The *Abrégé* was then inserted by Molinier in his *Pensées de Pascal*, Paris, 1889, v. **2**. A critical edition was given by Michaut, Librairie de l'Université, Fribourg (Switzerland), 1897. Molinier, then Michaut (open letter from Michaut to Molinier in *Revue Critique d'Histoire et de Littérature*, May 24, 1897, p. 414), have shown that Pascal was inspired by an ancient text; he followed closely the work of Jansen entitled *Series Vitae Jesu Christi juxta Ordinem Temporum*, published at the end of his *Tetrateuchus, sive Commentarius in Sancta Jesu Christi Evangelia*, authorization given at Louvain, May 10, 1639, published Paris, 1655, 586 p. in 4°. Brunschvicg, by a publication in extenso of the *Series Vitae Jesu Christi* of Jansen, accompanying the *Abrégé* of Pascal, *Œuvres*, v. **11**, 6ff., has shown not only that Pascal closely followed Jansen, but that he did so even when he was in disagreement with a similar work by Arnauld, *Historia et Concordia Evangelica*, Savreux, Paris, 1653, 445 pp. in 12°. (Cf. Introduction to the *Abrégé* : authenticity and sources, *Œuvres*, v. **11**, 3-6.)
98 *Œuvres*, Introduction to the *Abrégé*, v. **11**, 4.
99 *Œuvres*, v. **11**, 9.   100 *Œuvres*, v. **11**, 10, 11.
101 *Œuvres*, v. **11**, 11.   102 *Œuvres*, v. **11**, 13.   103 *Ibid.*
104 For example, from 50 to 81, *Œuvres*, v. **11**, 24-29.
105 Words restored by Faugère.   106 *Œuvres*, v. **11**, 72.
107 *Œuvres*, v. **11**, 94 (354).

V

1 *Lettres de Fermat à Pascal* (July 25, 1660) *et de Pascal à Fermat* (August 10, 1660), at the time of Pascal's stay in Auvergne, *Œuvres*, v. **10**, 1ff.
2 *Ibid.*, v. **10**, 4.
3 " Console thyself, thou wouldst not search for Me, hadst thou not found Me," *Le Mystère de Jésus*, *Œuvres*, v. **13**, 438.
4 Valéry, P., *Variation sur une " Pensée," La Revue Hebdomadaire*, No. 28, 32nd year, July 14, 1923, p. 170.
5 Boutroux, E., *Pascal*, collection *Les Grands Écrivains de la France*, 10th ed., Hachette, Paris, p. 5 [original edition, 1900].
6 Bergson started from the thesis of Boutroux, *De la Contingence des Lois de la Nature*, Baillière, Paris, 1874.
7 *Discours sur les Passions de l'Amour*, in *Des Pensées de Pascal*, by Victor Cousin, new edition, revised and enlarged, Ladrange, Paris, 1844, Appendix No. 11, p. 397.
8 The expression comes from Sophie Antoniadis, *Pascal Traducteur de la Bible*, Brill, Leyden, 1930, p. xv.
9 Clément Falcucci, in a thesis defended before the faculty of letters of the University of Paris in 1939 has shown well that Pascal, when he has once made up his mind for *true* conversion, fixes himself there, and when it is a question of judging men and situations, he returns to it constantly. [Falcucci, Cl., *L'Idée de Vérité chez Pascal*, Didier, Paris, Privat, Toulouse, 1939.]
10 *Vie par Mme Périer*, *Œuvres*, v. **1**, 102.   11 *Ibid.*, 104.

12   Giraud, V., *La Vie Héroïque de Blaise Pascal*, Crès, Paris, 1923.
13   Amiot, Ch.-G., *Impressions et Conclusions sur Pascal, La Revue Hebdomadaire*, No. 28, 32nd year, July 14, 1923, p. 299.
14   *Pensées*, Section iii, Fr. 210, *Œuvres*, v. 13, 128, 129.
15   Quoted in *Œuvres*, v. 1, 47.
16   *Mémoires* of Beurrier, II, 3, *Œuvres*, v. 10 391.
17   " *Der letzte Richter in allen Streitigkeiten ist nicht der Mensch, sondern Jener, der über den Menschen steht. Folglich muss man, um die Wahrheit zu finden, frei sein von dem, was die Menschen gemeinhin für die Wahrheit halten.*" (Schestow, L., *Die Nacht zu Gethsemane* [Pascals Philosophie], vom Verfasser durchgesehene Überstzung aus dem Russischen von Hans Ruoff, *Ariadne* Jahrbuch der Nietzsche-Gesellschaft, München, 1925 [36-109], 40.)
18   Vinet, A., *Etudes sur Blaise Pascal*, ed. Kohler, *cit.*, p. 10.
19   *Vie* par Mme Périer, *Œuvres*, v. 1, 96.
20   *Pensées*, Section x, Fr. 692, *Œuvres*, v. 14, 129, 130.
21   *Vie* par Mme Périer, *Œuvres*, v. 1, 91.
22   *Introduction à la Seconde Série des Œuvres de Pascal* [v. 4-11], v. 4, xxiii.
23   *Prière de Pascal pour demander à Dieu le Bon Usage des Maladies* (1659?), *Œuvres*, v. 9, 319ff.

With Mme Périer, Pascal's sister, Brunschvicg, and Bishop, we place this prayer in the last years of Pascal's life. The internal evidence—spiritual maturity of a text nourished with Biblical sustenance—appears decisive to us. The state of Pascal's health grew steadily worse toward 1657-1658. The *Prière* would then probably date from 1658 to 1662, and the fatigue following the controversy relative to the signature of the *Formulaire* and the death of Jacqueline (1661) inclines us to choose the last year of Pascal's life. We realize that this is an extreme solution.

24   Vinet, A., *Etudes sur Blaise Pascal*, ed. Kohler, *cit.*, p. 6.
25   *Mémoires* of Beurrier, II, 3, in *Œuvres*, v. 10, 391.

The sales of which Beurrier speaks here, " with the exception of the Bible, Saint Augustine, and very few other books," go back in part to January, 1655.

26   *Pensées*, Section vii, Fr. 550, *Œuvres*, v. 13, 432.
27   *Pensées*, Section vii, Fr. 553, *Œuvres*, v. 13, 440.
28   " *Man darf nicht ruhig sein, darf nicht schlafen.*" Schestow, L., *Die Nacht zu Gethsemane, Ariadne, op. cit.* (see our note 17), 101. The last paragraph of Schestow is superb.
29   *Introduction à la Seconde Série des Œuvres de Pascal* [v. 4-11], *Œuvres*, v. 4, lv.
30   Mauriac, F., *La Rencontre avec Pascal, La Revue Hebdomadaire, op. cit.*, 226.
31   *De Imitatione Christi*, III, liv, 18: " *Haec gratia* supernaturale lumen et quoddam *Dei* speciale *donum est*, et proprie electorum signaculum et pignus salutis aeterne."   32   *Pensées*, Section x, Fr. 670, *Œuvres*, v. 14, 106.
33   Du Bos, Ch., *Le Langage de Pascal, La Revue Hebdomadaire, op. cit.*, 261, 266.

See also *Port-Royal*, v. 3, 338, and the chapter entitled " The Prayer of Pascal," v. 4, of the *Histoire Littéraire du Sentiment Religieux en France*, by Bremond (*op. cit.*). Consult, also, of this last named author, the study *Pascal et l'Eglise Catholique, La Revue Hebdomadaire, op. cit.*, 171-183.

34   *Extrait d'une Lettre à M. et à Mlle de Roannez*, [November or December, 1656?], *Œuvres*, v. 6, 220, 221.

The Biblical allusions are to 1 Thessalonians v. 16-18; John xiv, 27; xvi. 22; and Matthew xiii. 44.

35   Bremond, H., *Histoire Littéraire du Sentiment Religieux en France, op.*

cit. The author, after asking himself if the Jansenist doctrine penetrated the interior life of Pascal (v. **4**, 319-322), discovers Pascal's joy and the egotistical character, according to him, of this joy, (v. **4**, 322-336) and concludes that there was no pessimism (v. **4**, 322, 323).

36   For example, Frs. 774-781, Section xii, *Œuvres*, v. **14**, 218-223.

37   *Pensées*, Fr. 515, Section vii, *Œuvres*, v. **13**, 414.

38   *Pensées*, Fr. 516, Section vii, *ibid.*   39   *Pensées*, Fr. 517, *ibid.*

40   *Le Mystère de Jésus, Pensées*, Fr. 553, Section vii, *Œuvres*, v. **13**, 438.

41   *Extrait d'une Lettre à M. et à Mlle de Roannez* (Sunday, November 5, 1656) *Œuvres*, v. **6**, 162, 163.

42   *Extrait d'une Lettre à M. et à Mlle de Roannez* (December, 1656?), *Œuvres*, v. **6**, 300, 299, 298.

43   Chevalier, J., *Des Rapports de la Vie et de la Pensée chez Pascal, La Revue Hebdomadaire, op. cit.*, p. 208.

44   *Pensées*, Section iv, Fr. 278, *Œuvres*, v. **13**, 201.

45   *Pensées*, Section viii, Fr. 568, *Œuvres*, v. **14**, 14, 15.

46   *Pensées*, Section x, Fr. 672, *Œuvres*, v. **14**, 107, 108.

47   Vinet, A., *Etudes sur Blaise Pascal*, ed. Kohler *cit.*, p. 153.

48   *Dix-septième Provinciale, Œuvres*, v. **6**, 343.

49   *Fragment d'une Lettre à M. et à Mlle de Roannez* (November, 1656?), *Œuvres*, v. **6**, 217.

50   Gibbons, James, Cardinal, *The Faith of Our Fathers*, 94th carefully revised and enlarged ed., Burns, Oates and Washbourne Ltd., London, ch. 7, " Infallible Authority of the Church," p. 65.

51   Lesêtre, H., *La Foi Catholique*, 27th ed., Beauchesne, Paris, 1923, p. 91.

52   Aigrain, R., in *Apologétique* [Catholic] published under the direction of Maurice Brillant and the Abbé M. Nédoncelle, Bloud et Gay, Paris, 1937, pp. 952, 953 [Nihil obstat, Paris, July 21, 1937—Imprimatur, Paris, July 23, 1937].   53   *Ibid.*, pp. 1017, 1018.

54   *Introduction aux* Pensées *de Pascal, Œuvres*, v. **12**, xiii.

55   *Lettre de la Sœur Jacqueline de Sainte-Euphémie Pascal à la Sœur Angélique de Saint Jean* (June 22-23, 1661), *Œuvres*, v. **10**, 105.

56   Blondel, M., *Le Jansénisme et l'Anti-Jansénisme de Pascal, Revue de Métaphysique et de Morale*, 30th year, No. 2, April-June, 1923, pp. 156, 157.

57   Jovy, E., *L'Almanach Spirituel de M. Pascal*, in *Etudes Pascaliennes, op. cit.*, v. **7**, 59.
     Jovy gives the facsimile of a page (v. **7**, 64).
     This almanac was edited and put in order by a penitent monk of the Third Order of Saint Francis, of the convent of Nazareth, near the Temple, at Paris—Father Martial, of Le Mans.   The said almanac had been appearing since 1646.

58   Gazier, A., *Les Derniers Jours de Blaise Pascal*, Champion, Paris, 1911, pp. 55, 64.   59   *Introduction aux* Pensées *de Pascal, Œuvres*, v. **12**, vii.

60   *Œuvres*, v. **10**, 372.   Cf. the complete publication of the record of the sickness and death of Pascal, *Œuvres*, v. **10**, 303-405.

61   *Œuvres*, v. **10**, 372.

62   Laporte, J., *Pascal et la Doctrine de Port-Royal, Revue de Métaphysique et de Morale, op. cit.*, p. 296.

63   Gazier, C., *Pascal et Port-Royal, La Revue Hebdomadaire, op. cit.*, p. 159.

64   Laporte, J., *op. cit.*, p. 304.

65   *Œuvres*, v. **1**, 46. (For the other letters, cf. **v. 1**, 44ff.)

66   Jovy, E., *Pascal Inédit., op. cit.*, **v. 2**, 454.

67   *Mémoires* of Beurrier, *Œuvres*, **v. 10**, 387.

68   MS. 4556, Mazarine Library, published as an appendix of Jovy, E., *Le Journal de M. de Saint-Gilles, Etudes Pascaliennes, op. cit.*, **v. 9**, 203, 204.

69   Bremond, H., *Pascal et l'Eglise Catholique, La Revue Hebdomadaire,* *op. cit.*, p. 174.

70   Jovy, E., *Un Temoignage Oublié du P. Thomassin sur Pascal* [work first given in the *Bulletin Historique et Scientifique d'Auvergne,* published by the Académie des Sciences, Belles-Lettres et Arts de Clermont-Ferrand, 2nd Series, No. 5, May, 1924], *Etudes Pascaliennes, op. cit.*, v. **3**, 41, 42.

71   It is thus that Reguron, *Pascal et l'Anti-Jansénisme* . . . , Grenoble, 1934, takes up again and develops the thesis of Chevalier on the evolution of the doctrine of Pascal who is said to have gone as far as positive anti-Jansenism; Kelly, H., in *Studies* (Dublin) for December, 1937, questions again the possibility of the retraction *in extremis*, et cetera.

72   Jovy, E., *Etudes Pascaliennes*, op. cit., **v. 5**, 11.

73   Bremond, H., *Pascal et l'Eglise Catholique, op. cit.*, 175.

74   Mauriac, F., *Blaise Pascal et sa Sœur Jacqueline,* Hachette, Paris, 1931, p. 226.   75   *Ibid.*, 231.   76   *Œuvres*, v. **1**, 113.

77   *Testament de Pascal* (August 3, 1662), *Œuvres*, v. **10**, 295.